SWIMMING POOLS

BY THE EDITORS OF
SUNSET BOOKS
AND
SUNSET MAGAZINE

SUNSET PUBLISHING CORPORATION, MENLO PARK, CALIFORNIA

We'd like to say thanks…
…to the many homeowners who welcomed us to their pools, and to the pool builders, architects, designers, and others who shared their expertise with us, helping to make this book possible.

Special thanks go to these individuals and firms: Cheryl R. Johnson, Advanced Technologies, Inc.; Fred Fritsinger, Aquarius Pools; Joel Grayson IV, Bio-Lab, Inc.; Donald G. Boos; Don Brandeau; Dick Wist, Brawner Pools; Henry Cole; Harold E. Matthews, Jr., CSM Master Pools; Mike Grisham, Fafco, Inc.; Reed Krumerie and Ken Thompson, Fox Pool Corp.; Rod Garrett; Jack DuPlessis, Hallmark Pool Corp.; Bill Kapranos; Jim Lefever; Al Stocking, Jr., Litehouse Pools; Richard Ketover, Major Pool Equipment Co.; Richard O. Carlson, Major Pools, Inc.; Frank Geremia and John Withers, Master Pools by Geremia; Marianne Kiernan, William P. Markert, Larry E. Paulick, Robert H. Steel, National Spa and Pool Institute; Duane Nelson and Ken Nelson, Nelson Aquatech Pools; Robert Maudsley, Peri-Bilt Pools; John R. Shelton, Shelton's Custom Pools; Doug Miller, Solar Industries, Inc.; Chris Hygelund, Sunsaver Pools; Brackston Whitaker, Whitaker Aquatech Pools.

Supervising Editor
Don Rutherford

Staff Editors
J. Anthony Dirksen
Donice G. Evans

Design
Joe di Chiarro

Illustrations
Bill Oetinger

Photography

Richard Fish: 45 bottom, 47 left, 49 bottom, 57 bottom, 58, 62 right, 68 left, 79. **Steve W. Marley:** 35, 38 bottom right, 39, 40, 41, 43, 48, 51 bottom, 55 top, 56, 59 top, 61 top, 63 right, 64 bottom, 65 bottom, 67 top left, 67 top right, 73 bottom, 75, 77. **Ells Marugg:** 36 left, 42 bottom. **Jack McDowell:** 33, 34, 37 top, 38 left, 42 top, 44, 45 top left, 45 top right, 46, 50 top, 52, 53, 54, 55 bottom left, 55 bottom right, 57 top, 59 bottom, 60, 61 bottom, 62 left, 63 left, 64 top, 65 top, 66, 67 bottom, 69 top, 70 top, 71, 72, 73 top, 74, 76, 78. **National Spa and Pool Institute:** 36 right, 37 bottom, 68 right, 70 bottom. **Don Normark:** 69 bottom. **Norman A. Plate:** 49 top. **Dennis Tromburg:** 47 right, 80. **Nikolay Zurek:** 50 bottom, 51 top.

Cover: Classic design in a compact site, rectangular pool with attached spa and cantilevered deck is a fun place to soak, sun, and splash. For another view of this pool, see page 73. Design: Robert Royston, Royston, Hanamoto, Alley & Abey. Photograph by Norman A. Plate. Cover design by Zan Fox.

Editor, Sunset Books: Elizabeth L. Hogan

Tenth printing October 1992

This publication was produced with the cooperation of the NSPI (National Spa and Pool Institute).

The NSPI is a trade association concerned with the quality of pool design and workmanship and the ethics of the pool industry.

CONTENTS

A PRIVATE POOL FOR YOU

Swimming pools are not new; the remains of 5000-year-old pools are still visible in India and Egypt. Yet never before have so many people enjoyed the benefits and pleasures of their own pools.

Whether you're seeking recreation, exercise, entertainment—or some combination of these—a glance at the pictures in this book, particularly those on pages 33–80, will surely whet your appetite for acquiring your own pool.

One benefit of pool ownership may not be immediately obvious. High fuel costs are forcing us to change our lifestyles and turn to more home-oriented recreation. As a center for family activities, a swimming pool is near ideal.

Your own private pool is always accessible day and night. Without burning gasoline and fighting traffic, you can use a recreation center that provides healthful and enjoyable exercise and fun.

And the expense of owning your own pool, an appreciating investment, is, in the long run, competitive with the expense of owning a boat or recreational vehicle, or taking your family on an annual two-week vacation.

If there's a swimming pool in your future, this book will supply the practical information you'll need to know how to select the right pool for your needs, how to go about having it installed and landscaped, and how to heat and maintain it. If you already own a pool, you'll find helpful information on maintaining and repairing your pool, installing alternate energy systems, and revitalizing what may by now be a tired and ailing pool.

FITTING YOUR POOL STYLE TO YOUR LIFE STYLE

Since a swimming pool can be a very permanent structure—as the remains of ancient pools in Asia, Africa, and Europe attest—you'll want to give a great deal of thought to the pool in your future before jumping in.

One of the first things you need to consider is how you will use a pool. You may want a spot where you—and even your children—can relax and entertain. Or you may see a pool as a healthful exercise center in your own backyard. For your children, a pool will be a playground or perhaps even a training center for aspiring swimming and diving champions.

Each use has certain requirements, and defining the uses now will help you choose the best location for your pool and acquire the style of pool that meets your needs (see "Which Pool for You?," page 15).

A pool used for relaxation and entertainment should have a large shallow area to splash around in, space around the pool for sunning, and room to set up tables and chairs nearby. The same pool will be great for children, too.

If you intend to swim for exercise or if your youngsters are Olympic hopefuls, your best choice will be a rectangular pool—the longer the better, and deep enough at both ends to negotiate turns safely.

Divers have very special requirements. In order for them to dive without injury, one end of the pool must have adequate depth, length, and width. The glare of the sun off the water can make it difficult for a diver to estimate the distance to the water surface and to the sides of the pool. If at all possible, orient the diving area so that at the time it's used the most, the sun will be behind the diver.

FINANCIAL ASPECTS OF POOL OWNERSHIP

In addition to deciding how you will use your pool, you need to consider the financial aspects of owning a pool—the effect of a pool on your property value, the expenses of maintaining your pool, and the legal responsibilities you'll incur as your new pool attracts friends, neighborhood kids, and even the friendly Labrador from next door.

Its effect on your property value

When you add a swimming pool to your property, the value of the property increases, though not necessarily dollar for dollar. Generally, as the home and land appreciates through the years, so does the pool.

The size, shape, and design of your pool can affect the ease with which you can sell your home. If the pool is esthetically pleasing and not highly specialized, you'll have a saleable home and pool combination.

Pool expenses

Though construction is usually the major cost of a pool, there are other ownership expenses.

Financing costs. If you elect to borrow money to build your pool, the interest on the loan can rival the cost of the pool, especially in times of unusually high interest rates. Interest paid is a deduction on your federal and most state tax returns.

Property taxes. Because a swimming pool generally increases the value of your property, you may see an increase in your property's assessed valuation, resulting in an increase in your property taxes.

Assessors, however, don't treat all types of pools in the same way. Their approach tends to be

based on the degree of permanence of the swimming pool.

In-ground pools are permanent structures and are taxed on the same basis as your home. On-ground pools are usually taxed as permanent structures; some communities, though, look on them as temporary and not subject to taxes. Above-ground pools, which can be dismantled and moved, are considered temporary and are not taxed by most communities. In areas where a pool can be used only for part of the year, the taxes may be reduced proportionately.

Insurance. The need for insurance protection begins when the first employee of the pool builder sets foot on your property. Though the contractor and his subcontractors should carry liability and property damage insurance, you'll want to check with your insurance agent before work begins to be sure you have adequate protection.

Owning a swimming pool can actually lower your fire insurance cost. If you live in an area where fire hazard is high, or where there is no municipal water supply, your pool will be a valuable source of water for fighting a fire.

Utility costs. You will require water to fill your pool, fuel to heat it—unless you use solar energy (see page 29)—and electricity to operate the filtration system.

You'll have to pay for water to fill your pool, unless your community allows pool owners a free fill. Expect a dramatic one-time increase in your water bill.

Gas, oil, or electricity to heat your pool will be the biggest utility expense. Rates for these fuels vary widely, depending on the type of fuel, your geographic location and climate, as well as the size, use, and water temperature of your pool. For suggestions on minimizing heating costs, see "The Solar-heated Pool," page 29, and "Energy-saving Suggestions," page 28.

The pump in the filtration system requires electricity, but the expense of running the pump will be significantly less than your heating

cost. The pool's size and water temperature, the area's climate and electric rates, and the length of time the filtration system must be operated will determine the cost.

To estimate your total utility costs, check with utility companies, pool builders, and pool-owning neighbors.

Pool maintenance. Routine maintenance of your pool will include keeping the water in proper chemical balance, maintaining the support equipment, and cleaning the pool surfaces.

You can contract with a pool service company to perform all these chores, or you can do them.

If you elect to do your own routine maintenance, your major expense will be for the chemicals used to maintain the chemical balance of the water. The cost of these chemicals depends on a number of widely variable factors—the pool size, the water temperature, the amount of time the pool is used, and the number of people using it.

Pool service companies, pool builders, and pool-owning neighbors can help you calculate the cost of maintaining your pool.

Responsibilities of a pool owner

The regulations and laws relating to an owner's responsibilities and liabilities vary from community to community and from state to state.

Your best assurance of safe operation is to comply with all of your community's zoning laws and health, safety, and building codes.

For additional protection, surround your pool area with a child-proof fence (one that has a self-closing, self-latching gate), mandatory in many communities. Make sure that young children using your pool are always supervised by a responsible adult. If you have a pool safety cover, keep it in place when the pool is not in use, and remove it completely when anyone is in the pool. Keeping the water clear and in proper chemical balance and the pool in a good state of repair will also help to ensure the safety of the swimmers.

CHOOSING A POOL SITE

I f the Roman pools of 2000 years ago are any indication, once your in-ground or on-ground pool is in place, it will be there for a long time. It makes sense to choose its location very carefully.

You can retain a professional to do the job for you. But you will be able to communicate your desires more easily if you first study the microclimates of your property, familiarize yourself with codes and other regulations, size up the landscape, and evaluate possible pool sites, particularly if your property has some unusual feature.

USING THE PROFESSIONAL

Architects, landscape architects and designers, soils and structural engineers, and pool and landscape contractors are among the professionals who can help you plan your pool.

Architects & landscape architects

Many homeowners retain an architect or landscape architect for projects involving a pool and the surrounding environment. These professionals are state licensed and are trained to create designs that are structurally sound, functional, and esthetically pleasing. In addition, they are familiar with construction methods and materials, understand the mechanics of estimating, and can negotiate with and supervise the contractor.

Landscape designers

Landscape designers usually have the education and training of landscape architects but are not state licensed. Some landscape designers are licensed contractors, however, and can both design the landscaping for your pool and perform the actual work.

Soils & structural engineers

If you are planning a pool on an unstable or steep lot, your building department may require that you (or your landscape architect) consult with soils and structural engineers and obtain engineering reports.

Soils engineers evaluate soil conditions on a proposed construction site and establish design specifications for foundations that can resist whatever stresses unstable soil exerts.

Structural engineers, often working with the site evaluation and calculations provided by a soils engineer, design pools and foundations for other structures.

Pool & landscape contractors

Pool contractors specialize in pool construction and landscape contractors in garden construction. Both are state licensed. Some also have design skills and experience; their fees for designing usually are included in the price bid for performing the work. Though the design skills of some contractors may be limited, many award-winning pools have been designed by major pool contractors.

Pool and landscape contractors are responsible for hiring qualified workers or subcontractors, ordering materials, scheduling work, and seeing that the job is completed according to the contract.

Choosing a professional

The best way to choose a professional is to collect recommendations from pool owners and inspect the person's work. If you don't have someone in mind, look in the Yellow Pages under "Architects," "Landscape Architects," "Landscape Designers," "Landscape Contractors," and "Swimming Pool Contractors."

Though some excellent professionals have no professional affiliation, many belong to the American Society of Landscape Architects (ASLA), the American Institute of Architects (AIA), the National Spa and Pool Institute (NSPI), or other organizations. To locate members in your area, contact a nearby office.

RESTRICTIONS, CODES & OTHER REGULATIONS

Building a swimming pool—like any other addition or alteration to your property—brings a myriad of legal requirements set forth in deed restrictions, zoning laws, and building, health, and safety codes. Take the time to look into *all* of these *before* you commit yourself to installing a pool. When you design landscaping for your pool (see page 90), remember that additions such as fences, decks, and gazebos must conform, too.

Deed restrictions

Somewhere in the deed to your property you may find restrictions that could affect the design and location of your pool and poolside structures. These restrictions may bind you to rules set by a homeowners' association or provide for a utility easement or right-of-way under, over, or through your property.

Though the rules of a homeowners' association can be changed by vote of the members, deed restrictions can be changed only by mutual agreement among all parties bound by the restrictions or by court action.

Zoning laws

These city or county laws govern land use—yours included. They can determine where you can place your pool, how close to the property lines you can build, and how large you can make your poolside structures.

Zoning laws usually have provisions for the granting of variances. If you can show that meeting the precise requirements of the laws would create an "undue hardship," and that you would not be encroaching on the privacy of your

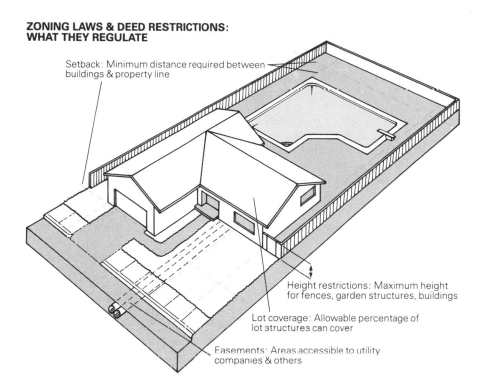

ZONING LAWS & DEED RESTRICTIONS: WHAT THEY REGULATE

Setback: Minimum distance required between buildings & property line

Height restrictions: Maximum height for fences, garden structures, buildings

Lot coverage: Allowable percentage of lot structures can cover

Easements: Areas accessible to utility companies & others

neighbors, a hearing officer or zoning board of appeals can grant you a variance. Application must be made through your local building or planning department.

Building codes

Aimed at protecting you from faulty construction methods, these codes set minimum standards for design, construction, and materials used in building. Some communities have specific codes for pools; others apply the requirements of the regular building code.

Though most local codes are patterned after one of the national codes, communities can modify or add to these standards to satisfy local needs. For example, some communities do not allow vinyl-lined pools; others ban one-piece fiberglass pools. Check with your building department early in the planning stage—your pool options may be fewer than were at first apparent.

Health & safety codes

Your community may have specific laws covering such facets of pool ownership as water quality, life-

saving equipment, and protective fences and gates. Some communities incorporate provisions for pool construction in the health and safety code, not in the building code; you need to consult both your local health and building departments to determine pool requirements and the jurisdiction each department has in pool construction and operation.

Additional regulations

Drought, an energy shortage, a pool accident, or some other crisis often prompts additional government control. Local and state government agencies have considered
• restricting the use of water for filling pools
• banning the use of natural gas for heating pools
• mandating solar heating for all new pools
• banning a specific type of swimming pool
• requiring that covers be sold with new pools
• requiring fencing and self-closing gates around pools.

Utility companies and building and planning departments can tell you about any restrictions currently applicable in your community.

CLIMATE, WEATHER & YOUR POOL

Though official climate and weather records can help determine the average length of the swimming season in your area, it's the day-to-day weather on *your* property that will determine your poolside comfort.

Since the warmth or coolness of your pool will be decided largely by its orientation, it's wise to study the microclimates of your property along with the regional climate and weather. Buildings, trees, or other obstructions on or near your property can have an effect on the amount of sunlight and wind your property receives.

A pool in almost any location may serve well in midsummer, but wise planning can extend the outdoor season by several weeks, or even months.

The general outlook

If you've lived in your present area a number of years, you should have a feeling for the general climate in terms of average seasonal air temperatures, rain and/or snowfall patterns, prevailing wind directions, and number of sunny days.

It not, you can get climate information from the National Oceanic and Atmospheric Administration (NOAA, pronounced "Noah"), National Climatic Center, Asheville, NC 28801. Request the current annual issue of the Local Climatological Data for your area.

You also may be able to get accurate climate and weather information through U.S. Weather Bureau offices, public power and utility companies, meteorology departments on college and university campuses, and agricultural extension offices.

No matter how much official information you gather, take personal stock of the local weather as well as you can. Your neighborhood almost certainly will vary somewhat from the recording stations. And by all means talk with the "old-timers"

in your neighborhood. They can extend your knowledge of the local climate by many years.

Sun & shade

Observing and recording the patterns of sunlight and shade created on your property by the sun as it passes across the sky will help you place your pool so as to make maximum use of the available sunlight during swimming hours.

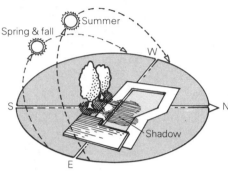

Sun at noon

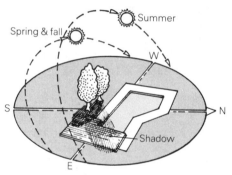

Sun at 4 P.M.

Changing shadows during day and in different seasons affect amount of sunlight on pool site.

Theoretically a pool with a southern exposure (in the northern hemisphere) will be warmer than one that faces north. A west-facing pool will be warmer than one with an eastern exposure. And a pool facing south will be warmer than one facing west.

There are exceptions to this rule, though. In desert areas, where noontime temperatures can be extremely high for several months during the year, a north-facing pool can hardly be considered cold. In some coastal areas, on the other hand, a south or west-facing pool can be cold because of ocean winds and chilly fogs in summer.

Consider the wind

Wind is almost as important a factor in selecting a pool site as the sun. Too much wind blowing across a pool area on a temperate day can be unpleasant, as can no breeze at all on a hot summer day. Wind can draw heat from the pool and evaporate water and chemicals, adding to your operating expenses.

Place the pool where it uses the winds to the best advantage; then control the wind, if necessary, with fences, screens, trees, or plants.

The wind can affect two houses on a hill in different ways (see below). The house on top of the hill is exposed to the full sweep of the wind which can even eddy down behind it, causing problems for a pool owner. The wind is diverted and dispersed by the grove of trees on the lower lot. A pool behind this house will be almost totally protected from wind and won't need additional screening.

Three wind systems—prevailing, diurnal (daily), and irregular, high-velocity winds—can have an effect on your poolside comfort.

Prevailing winds. In some parts of the world, like the trade wind belt, the prevailing wind blows constantly for weeks or even months without letup. In the United States, prevailing winds are felt only in Hawaii, in the high mountains of the West, and in parts of the Great Plains states.

Diurnal or daily winds. Fortunately, these winds—very important in choosing a pool site—are predictable. Some of them are most prevalent during the swimming season.

In coastal areas and on the shores of large lakes, the still air of morning gradually gives way to increasingly strong breezes from the water during the afternoon. These onshore winds die down when the sun sets. By early evening, the air flow has reversed. In some areas, these afternoon sea breezes, approaching gale force, swoop down over the coastal mountains and make most pool activity impossible without adequate wind screens.

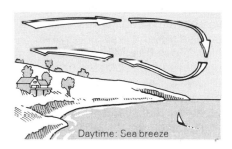
Daytime: Sea breeze

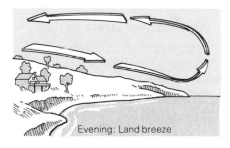
Evening: Land breeze

Inland mountain areas also experience reversible daily winds. Generally, the air flow is upslope during the day and downslope after sunset. Near the entrances to

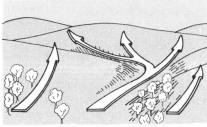
Daytime: Upslope breeze

canyons and valleys, the evening breezes can be quite strong and cool.

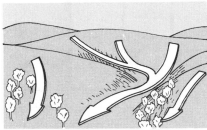
Evening: Downslope breeze

Irregular, high-velocity winds. Meteorologists call these winds "foehns" (pronounced *ferns*), but residents know them under various local names—chinooks, boras, Santa Anas, or Boulder winds. They flow downslope or out of mountain basins. Though these winds are usually hot and dry, in some areas they feel cool relative to the local air; in the Pacific Northwest, the foehn can be moist.

Many of these winds occur in winter, but in Southern California the Santa Ana can blow for days during summer and autumn.

SIZING UP THE LANDSCAPE

Sizing up your property on a plot plan that catalogs both assets and liabilities will help you find the best site for your pool. Your plan should include everything you know and can learn about your property—sun and wind patterns, codes and restrictions, contour and condition of the land, and location of utility lines, trees, and access.

Making a plot plan

You will find it easier to evaluate the placement of various sizes and shapes of pools in your home-garden environment if you work with a plan showing all the features of your property. Later on, you can use the plan to draw in decks and other structures, as well as landscaping and lighting.

Your scale drawing (see next page) should be on graph paper with provision for overlay sheets of tracing paper. The tracing paper allows you to sketch ideas for pools one after another without redrawing the base each time.

You'll save hours of complicated measuring if you can obtain copies of a surveyor's plot plan, architect's drawings or house plans, and contour maps that illustrate vital statistics of lot and buildings.

Plot plans (surveyor's drawings) usually locate your property and show streets, property corners, and distances between corners, plus the locations of any structures on the site when the lot was surveyed. Available through your county recorder or title company, these plans make an excellent starting point for your base map; simply transfer information from the plot plan to your graph paper.

Architect's drawings usually show site plan, floor plan, elevations, and foundation details.

Contour maps show the slope of the land with a series of lines, each separated from the next by a fixed difference in elevation—especially helpful if you are building a pool on a hillside lot. Ask for contour maps in the city or county engineer's office or in the department of public works.

Drawing the plan. You'll need graph paper (about 24 by 36-inch sheets, 4 or 8 squares to the inch), pencils, erasers, and a ruler. For your drawing, use the largest scale the graph paper will allow.

On 24 by 36-inch graph paper with a scale of ¼ inch per foot (4-squares-to-the-inch paper), you can draw a lot that measures about 90 by 140 feet. Using a scale of ⅛ inch per foot (8-squares-to-the-inch paper), you can cover a lot measuring 180 by 280 feet.

Your plot plan should show the following features:
• dimensions of your lot
• location of your house on the lot, as well as doors and windows and the rooms from which they open
• location of decks, patios,

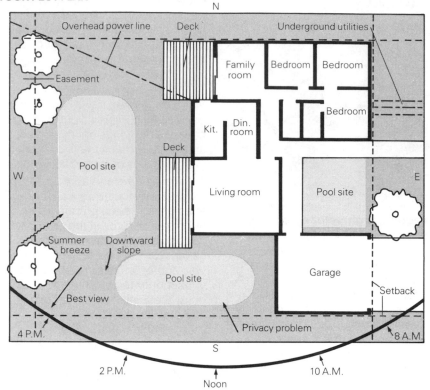

Use a plan showing all features of your lot to determine location, size, and shape of your pool.

walks, fences, walls, and other structures
 • points of the compass—north, east, south, and west
 • location of easements or other rights-of-way contained in your deed
 • utility lines—underground gas, water, sewer, electric, telephone, and television lines and the depth of each (check with the appropriate utility company); overhead electric, telephone, and television lines and the height of each (it's dangerous to locate a pool under wires carrying electricity); septic tanks, leaching fields, and propane gas tanks; exterior outlets for water and electricity; meter boxes and air conditioning units you may want to screen
 • sun and wind patterns
 • potential problems beyond the lot lines that might affect sun, view, or privacy—tall trees or a neighbor's second story windows, for example
 • front, side, and backyard setback boundaries
 • contours of your lot (if you don't

have a contour map, mark high and low spots, direction of slopes, and natural drainage patterns)
 • natural features, such as rock outcrops, soil types, or wet spots.

Access for the contractor

Before excavation can begin, you must provide adequate access for heavy equipment. The minimum width for access to the pool site is about 8 feet, though 10 feet is preferable. Sometimes, small equipment can enter through a space only 5 feet wide, but because excavation will take longer, the cost will be higher. If equipment cannot be brought in, the pool must be hand dug at a prohibitive cost.

As an alternative, you may be able to bring in the equipment over a neighbor's property, but you, not the pool builder, must make the arrangements.

You may have to remove fences and gates. If heavy equipment will cross a curb, sidewalk, patio, or lawn, take measures to

prevent damage. These, too, will be your responsibilities.

Though you don't want to build your pool over a gas or water main or under a power line, your pool site should have ready access to them. Some pool contracts require additional payment for runs to these utility lines over some minimum distance. A reliable and knowledgeable builder, however, should include these costs in the bid.

Trees & shrubs

Generally, it's preferable not to build a pool near trees and large shrubs. Leaves, blossoms, and fruit dropping near and in the pool will add to your cleaning chores. And a tall tree or shrub may shade your pool just at the time you'll be using it.

If there are trees or shrubs that you want to keep, try to locate your pool so that the prevailing winds blow the debris away from the pool. In addition, plot the shadows thrown by the trees; then determine whether or not you would welcome that shade in and around your pool during the swimming season.

Assessing pool views

Pleasure, privacy, and safety are concerns when you choose a pool location. When seen from inside your home, the pool should be an attractive part of the landscape. On the other hand, the view from a neighbor's upstairs window may infringe on your privacy. And if there's a beautiful view from your property, position the pool so you can enjoy the view from poolside.

If children will use your pool, you either need a clear view of their activities from the house or, as in the case of small children, you will have to be at poolside when they're swimming.

Mark the fields of view on an overlay of your plot plan. If you've already decided on a potential site, use an enlarged plan of the proposed pool area to mark the fields; you will want a large plan when you come to consider landscaping.

Slope, soil & drainage

Ideally, you want a pool site that's level and slightly higher than the land around it. The underlying soil should be stable and easy to dig. Also, you'll need a dry site, with good surface and subsurface drainage. Good drainage conditions will depend on the slope of the land and the nature of the soil.

Slope. By analyzing a contour map of your lot, you can determine where the land slopes and how steep the slopes are. You should also be able to locate any high spots, depressions, flat areas, or drainage paths. If you don't have a contour map, wander around your property and take note of any of these features; then mark them on your plot plan.

While you're at it, take a look on the far side of any fences. One might conceal a gully that could turn your sparkling pool into a muddy mess during a storm.

Even if your property has no ideal level area, remember that hillsides can become sites for magnificent swimming pools. Turn to page 12 for some solutions to hillside building problems.

Soil. Because soil conditions not only affect the ease of excavating for a pool but also have the potential for damaging or even destroying a pool shell, you must determine the type of soil underlying your property.

Once you've zeroed in on a possible pool site, you can have the precise nature of your soil identified—have a hole dug to pool depth. Some soil types require special design features in the pool. Though the pool contractor may have had experience with these conditions, you may want to consult a soils engineer (see page 6).

Loam, commonly called "garden soil," is ideal for a pool site in many parts of the country since it's easy to dig. The walls of the excavation will be stable and not likely to collapse. In other areas, though, it may settle or compact causing damage to the pool shell.

Sandy soil, the bane of pool builders, usually caves in during excavation. Because the walls must be shored up with wood or sprayed with concrete to prevent collapse, the construction cost is increased. Sometimes, a concrete pool in sandy soil must be built with a thicker shell or supported on piers or pilings.

Wet soil, whether waterlogged from surface runoff or in an area with a high water table, is best avoided, if at all possible. Excavating for a pool in wet soil is very expensive. And the pressure of the underground water can collapse an empty pool built in such soil, or float the pool out of the ground.

Expansive soil, known as "adobe" in the West, becomes a problem only when a significant amount of water percolates into the ground. The pressure exerted on the sides of even a filled pool can cause it to collapse.

Some communities ban types of pools that cannot be reinforced to withstand the pressure of wet expansive soil. A concrete pool in expansive soil may have to be built with a thicker shell; it may also require expansion joints between the shell and coping (the lip around the edge of the pool), the coping and deck, and within the deck. A trench dug around the pool 5 to 10 feet from the walls and filled with loose material can help absorb the soil expansion. Surface drainage must be directed away from the pool area and any drainage lines must be leakproof.

Corrosive soil is no longer a serious problem, now that plastic pipe has replaced metal pipe in swimming pool construction.

Though metal pools and the metal wall panels used with some vinyl-lined pools are treated against corrosion, special precautions may be required in highly corrosive soil. Your pool contractor or soils engineer should be aware of any problems in your area.

Rock, sometimes visible as outcroppings but usually hidden beneath the soil, requires expensive drillings and blasting. If rock under-lies the site you must use, consider building a vinyl-lined on-ground pool without a hopper or deep end (see page 19).

Filled ground is unsuitable as a pool site unless the soil was compacted properly (this is difficult to assess) or unless the bottom of the pool will be deeper than the disturbed soil.

The weight of a filled pool built on improperly compacted fill compresses the soil and allows the pool to settle into the ground. If it settles evenly, the shell can pull away from the deck or, in the case of a concrete pool, from the bond beam. Uneven settling can crack the shell of a concrete pool. An expensive solution is to support the pool shell on piers or pilings that sit on solid ground.

Even though you may not see evidence of fill, dig some test holes on your potential sites. If you find layers of different kinds of soil or any manmade debris, you can be sure that the area was filled.

Drainage. Usually, natural drainage on the surface of your property or a neighbor's property can be diverted from a pool site; disposing of underground water and pool water is another story entirely.

Surface drainage need not be a problem if you avoid building your pool in a low-lying area from which water cannot drain. During storms, muddy water collecting there can spill over into your pool.

Water running off a slope or down a natural drainage path can fill your pool with mud and debris. If you cannot find a site free from runoff, you can landscape the pool area to divert the water .

Subsurface drainage problems—water accumulating just under the surface of your site, or a spring running under your property —may not make a site unusable, but the excavation will be more expensive; in addition, a drainage system may have to be installed under the pool to carry away the water.

Sometimes, a soggy low spot or especially lush vegetation will alert you to an area of poor underground drainage on your property. Most of the time, though, the condition is hidden until you dig a test hole or start excavating your pool.

Ask your pool-owning neighbors if they encountered any subsurface drainage problems; you can also consult local soils engineers, pool contractors, and building inspectors.

Pool water drainage involves disposing of the pool water if you have to drain it, and disposing of the water from the filter when it is serviced. Dumping 30,000 gallons of chlorinated pool water in your garden would kill all your plants—not to mention the damage it would inflict on your neighbor's yard.

If your community prohibits emptying pool water into the sewer or storm drain system, you may have to construct a dry well to absorb the water.

RULES-OF-THUMB FOR CHOOSING THE SITE

Even if you think of your lot as the size of a postage stamp, you may have more than one possible site for your pool—behind the house, in the side yard (a lap pool might fit), or even in the front yard.

To help you evaluate various pool sites and select the best one for your needs, here's a check list of desirable features in a pool site:
• sun on the pool area all day long, unless you live in the desert Southwest, and need some shade in the middle of the day
• shelter from all but the gentlest of breezes, except for desert areas, where some wind is welcome because of its cooling effect
• easy access for the heavy equipment used by the pool contractor
• convenience to utility lines—gas, water, and electricity
• trees and shrubs located so as not to dirty the pool but to make the best use of the sun

• easily and pleasantly viewed from the house
• shielded from the view of neighbors
• roomy enough for poolside activities—diving, sunning, and entertaining
• convenient for swimmers but located so they don't leave wet footprints on the living room carpet when they go in to change.

Because you're not likely to find a site that meets all these requirements, you'll have to compromise to find the best combination for your needs.

You might have to sacrifice a site that's perfectly framed in the living room window for a location that makes the pool visible from the kitchen window—a desirable feature if you have children. By moving the pool closer to some trees you might trade off more pool cleaning work for increased privacy from your neighbors.

In a windy area where compromise is not possible, shielding the pool with shrubs, trees, or a wind screen can be a solution.

As you evaluate pool sites, you'll want to consider different sizes, shapes, and types of pools (see "Which Pool for You?," page 15). Though you won't want to landscape until your pool is built, giving some thought now to at least the major landscape elements—decks, fences, trees, and shrubs—will help assure that your pool fits in with the overall landscape (see "Landscaping Your Pool," page 90).

For many lots, deciding where to place the pool is obvious. For others, because of size, shape, terrain, or a number of other factors, the choice is much more difficult. The section that follows illustrates some typical and some not-so-typical pool and lot combinations.

LOTS WITH A CHALLENGE

Because of their shape, some lots demand special attention from the

pool builder or designer. Though the challenge of the hillside or unusually shaped lot is obvious, creating a unique pool and landscape environment on a typical rectangular suburban lot also requires careful consideration.

If your lot falls into the category of a challenging site, take heart from the suggestions and examples that follow. You'll also want to thumb through the succeeding chapters—they'll stimulate your imagination toward finding a solution to your particular situation.

Hillside lots

Designing and building on a hillside requires the services of experts. The steeper the hillside, the more important these experts are. The angle of the slope, the nature and stability of the soil, the design of the pool shell, and the method of anchoring the shell to the slope all must be considered.

Despite the problems, a hillside can allow a designer to create a magnificent pool not possible on a flat site. The pool can appear to soar into space or be nestled in a grove of trees. A hillside can host a pool on land that was previously unusable. Few hillsides are too steep for a pool builder—pools have even been suspended from the edges of cliffs.

A hillside pool needs to withstand earth pressure on one side and have well-engineered support on the other. Downslope supports for the pool should be built on a solid foundation, preferably rock. Retaining walls on the upslope side, sometimes incorporating the pool structure itself, must be sufficient to contain a possible earth or loose-rock slide.

Surface water must be routed from the hill around the pool to a lower slope, and decks must be designed to prevent water from seeping into the ground near the pool.

Depending on the lot, you may be limited in the choice of pool size, shape, and type of construction. Take the time to seek out companies and contractors with a reputation for tackling tough problems.

A report from a soils engineer and the services of a structural engineer may be required (see page 6).

Pool access and adequate decking can be a challenge. It's a good idea to plan the area completely on paper, including all steps, decking, and structures. If the site is too confined, a pool may be impractical.

Finally, consider costs. The additional expense of building a pool on a steep hillside can equal and even exceed the cost of the pool. But if your lot is not excessively steep, expect only a moderate increase in cost.

Illustrated below are some examples of how pools can be built on a reasonably steep hillside. You'll find other examples on pages 44–46.

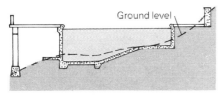

Concrete pool on grade

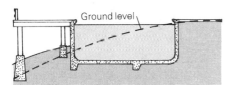

Concrete pool built into hill

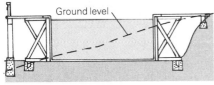

Vinyl-lined pool built into hill

The standard lot

Because of the sameness in both the style of the houses and the shape of the lots in suburban housing developments, there is a tendency for the landscaping to conform to a neighborhood norm.

To show that it is possible to be original and creative even on the small, rectangular suburban lot, we have created four pool and landscape schemes. Though the lot and house are the same, each pool and garden is unique.

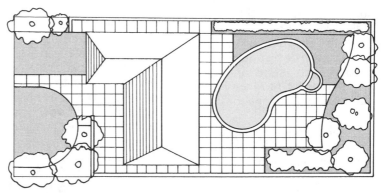

Free form pool, backed by grove of trees, lends feeling of graceful informality.

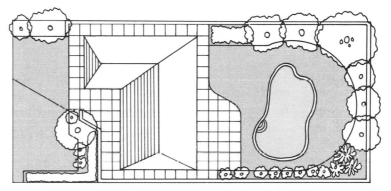

Naturalistic pool in sylvan glade creates a forest setting in a small garden.

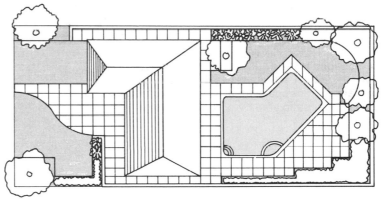

Angular pool and geometric shapes produce a strikingly contemporary environment.

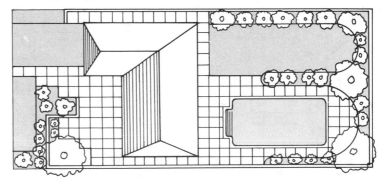

Rectangular pool adjacent to spacious, sheltered lawn divides lot into two separate activity areas.

Lots with unusual shapes

An unusually shaped lot might at first look like a liability, but it can often be just the opposite. A little imagination used in designing and placing a pool can transform an awkwardly shaped lot into a very functional and appealing environment.

On a square-shaped lot, shown at right, an elliptical pool relieves the strong angular lines of the house and lot. To make the yard look longer, design focal points at each end—a small, intimate garden tucked into one corner and a cabana beyond the pool in the other corner.

The primary drawbacks to the wedge-shaped lot shown below are its sharply angled corners and unequally divided outdoor spaces. These become assets in a design which provides spaces for a large, angular pool, a private patio area, and a small garden. Trees beyond the pool conceal it from neighbors views and mask the sharp corner.

Study these approaches—they make good use of space available for a pool on four typical lots with unusual shapes. They're not the only solutions, but they do illustrate how effective design can minimize eccentric features in the landscape.

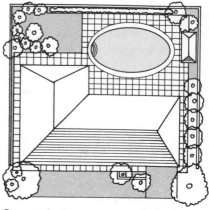

Square lot's severe angularity is softened with elliptical pool; focal points at either end of garden extend space. From house, one may look left toward an intimate garden (accessible from main patio or master bedroom) or right across pool to cabana.

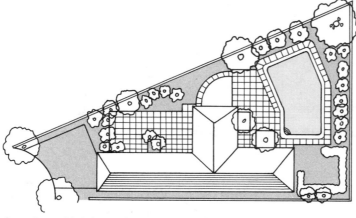

On wedge-shaped lot, irregular outdoors spaces lend themselves to distinct activity zones. Generous pool area in one corner provides space for all kinds of pool-related activities. Smaller patio area near front is private and intimate.

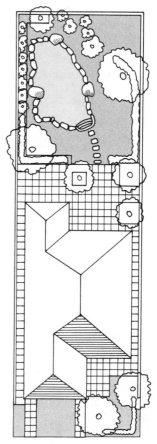

Barber-pole look of long, narrow lot is relieved by dividing space into two distinct, offset areas. Here, the eye is carried on an arc across the large patio area into the woodsy and secluded glade with its naturalistic pool.

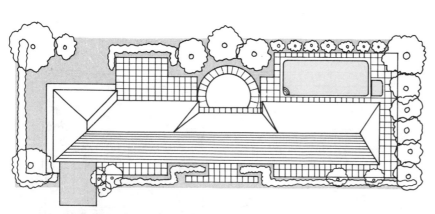

Deepen an extremely shallow lot by creating a number of focal points across width of garden, a central rounded patio ringed with trees, a rectangular pool and spa on one side, and an entertainment terrace on the other.

WHICH POOL FOR YOU?

There are no easy answers to the question of which size, shape, and type of pool construction best meets your needs. Many factors will influence your decisions—personal tastes, pool use, the conditions of the site, the types of construction available in your area, and, of course, your budget.

Fitting your pool to your budget

Though your budget may impose limitations, begin by planning the pool and surroundings you'd most like to have. Then obtain bids and you'll know exactly what your dream will cost. That's the time for you and your contractor to concentrate on bringing your pool project within the limits of your budget.

Often, the solution is to defer parts of the project. Because you planned both the pool and the surroundings, you can eliminate those parts of the project that can be added later with the least amount of increased cost.

A gazebo or an outdoor shower, for instance, can be added any time—the only increased cost will be that due to inflation. On the other hand, underwater lighting, easily installed when the pool is being built, is a costly and involved project if added a few years later.

The only absolute about the costs of the various pool types is that the portable above-ground pool with a vinyl liner is considerably less expensive than any type of permanent pool construction.

The cost of a permanent pool varies widely, depending on a number of factors—size, shape, type and quality of construction, location, and the competitive situation among local pool builders.

Of the two most popular types of pools built in the United States— the air-sprayed concrete pool and the vinyl-lined pool—the concrete pool is the more expensive. Though the difference is not great in the sunbelt states, it is in the colder northern climes, where more steel reinforcing rods and a thicker concrete shell are needed to withstand frost pressure. In addition, builders of concrete pools must contend with a shorter building season in the colder areas.

If you want to build your own

Building your own pool is a major project that requires a lot of hard work and skill, especially for plumbing and electrical installation; otherwise, you'll have to subcontract parts of the work. If you're inclined to do it, consider a vinyl-lined pool (see page 19) or a portable pool (see page 20).

You'll find manufacturers and dealers who will cater to your needs, supplying complete packages that contain everything you need except water. Detailed instructions are part of the package. Even so, you may want to hire professional supervision supplied by the dealer or manufacturer, and you'll almost certainly want to contract out such heavy work as excavation and backfilling.

DETERMINING SIZE & SHAPE

Site conditions and landscape requirements will affect your decision on the size and shape of your pool. But personal tastes and the ways in which you will use your pool are the most important considerations.

Your personal needs

The architectural axiom that form follows function applies particularly to a pool's size and shape. A family of happy frolickers needs a pool with a large shallow area. Lap swimmers require a pool that has a long, straight section with parallel ends. And divers must have a pool long, wide, and deep enough for safe diving.

If your family includes all of these, choose a pool that can accommodate all types of swimming and diving. For example, the shallow, short leg of an L-shaped pool can be large enough for the frolickers, and the other leg can be long enough for the lap swimmers and, at one end, deep and wide enough for the divers.

In considering the pool options and requirements for divers, become familiar with the booklet "Suggested Minimum Standards for Residential Swimming Pools" published by the National Spa and Pool Institute, 2000 K Street, N.W., Washington, DC 20006. (The NSPI is a trade association concerned with the quality of pool design and workmanship and the ethics of the pool industry.)

For frolickers. Many pool users splash and play in shallow water and do little, if any, swimming. For this purpose, figure a minimum depth of 33 inches, increasing to 4 or 5 feet. Any size and shape will do, even a converted wine tank (see pages 48 and 49).

Though you may have small children, don't be tempted to include a wading pool. They would soon outgrow it and be enjoying themselves in the main part of the pool with the rest of the family. Build a separate wading pool that later can be converted into a garden pond. Or buy a small, inexpensive plastic wading pool.

For lap swimmers. Serious swimmers need a pool that's at least 3½ to 4 feet deep so they don't touch bottom while swimming and so they can safely negotiate turns at each end. The pool should have parallel ends and be straight and long—the longer, the better.

If the pool will be a training center for competitive swimmers, make the length an even divisor of 75 feet—25 or 37½ feet. Then they can develop a style usable for competitive meets.

Width is not critical—some lap pools in side yards are just wide enough for one swimmer. Keep in mind, though, that such a highly specialized pool may not meet the needs of potential purchasers of your home if you decide to sell.

There is an alternative if you're a serious swimmer with neither the space nor the desire for a long pool.

You can exercise by swimming against a current generated by a separate pumping system (see page 78).

For divers. Small pools are dangerous for diving, as the risk of hitting one's head on the bottom or the sides is great. According to the minimum standards suggested by NSPI (see above), diving from a height of only 20 inches above the water requires a pool at least 28 feet long, 15 feet wide, and 7½ feet deep at the deep end. Other requirements for the size and contours of pools used for diving are also outlined in the NSPI booklet.

Pool size

Well over half the pools built in the United States in recent years have ranged from 450 square feet (15 by 30 feet) to 800 square feet (20 by 40 feet). In 1979, though, a continuing decline in the proportion of pools less than 450 square feet was reversed.

Another trend, at least in some parts of the country, is to flat-bottomed pools with a water depth of 4 feet. Pools with a depth of about 3 feet at each end and 6 feet in the middle are popular also. Except for diving, a deep section is unnecessary.

Industry members observing these trends attribute them not to lower costs, but rather to smaller lots, condominium and townhouse living, and economy of operation and maintenance. A small pool requires less water and chemicals, is cheaper to filter and heat, and takes less effort to maintain. And small can be beautiful, too, as some of the pools in "A Color Gallery of Pools" (pages 33–80) illustrate.

Though the trend is to smaller pools, large ones still dominate the market. Most experts agree that a pool measuring at least 16 by 32 feet, with a deep end for diving, is needed for a full range of swimming activities.

Unless your pool site strictly limits the pool size, one way to determine your needs is to allow 36 square feet for each swimmer and

100 square feet for each diver. If you predict that 10 people, including three divers, will use your pool on a busy afternoon, figure on a pool with an area of 552 square feet or 16 by 35 feet.

Pool shape

The simpler the shape of your pool, the better it will blend into a landscaped setting and enhance the appearance of your property. Shapes developed from squares, rectangles, circles, ovals, and other simple geometric figures will not compete with the landscaping. Nor do such shapes require great design ability.

A truly naturalistic pool is also simple in shape because forms in nature are simple. But making it so much a part of nature that there is hardly any delineation between pool and nature usually requires the skill of a top landscape architect. A naturalistic pool is not easy to integrate into a residential lot and will probably be more expensive.

Unusual shapes are difficult to landscape well because they compete with the other elements in your landscape. But sometimes an unusual shape is the best choice. If your lot is small and wedge-shaped, your pool may also have to be wedge-shaped. Or to save a tree or other natural feature that's valuable to you, you may decide to bend in one side of a pool. You may even want a pool shape that relates to a special interest, such as the one on page 57 in the shape of a music note.

Space around the pool

Since your pool will become the focus for outdoor activities and entertainment, you'll want to make sure your design provides enough space around the pool for swimmers and nonswimmers alike.

Except in the case of a naturalistic pool, you will want a paved area or deck at least 3 feet wide on all sides of the pool. This deck allows swimmers convenient access to the pool, keeps mud and dirt out of the water, prevents the garden

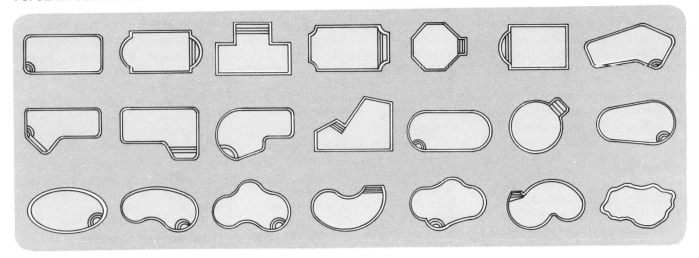

from becoming waterlogged, and permits the person cleaning the pool to work unhindered.

With naturalistic pools, all other considerations are secondary to appearance. Some owners, though, may naturalize only part of the area around the pool, reserving the rest for casual enjoyment.

For complete comfort, sitters, loungers, and sun bathers need a minimum space of about 3 by 6 feet apiece and at least 3 feet between one another. For a table and four chairs, you'll want an area measuring at least 10 by 10 feet.

One rule of thumb states that the area for poolside activities should be at least equal to the area of the pool. For example, a 20 by 40 foot pool (800 square feet) with the minimum 3-foot-wide deck on three sides would have an activity area 12 feet wide along one of the long sides.

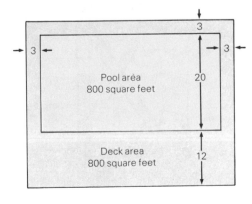

Divers, too, have their poolside requirements. Depending on its length, the diving board can extend as much as 10 feet onto the deck from the edge of the pool; the divers will need at least 2 more feet to walk around the end of the board. And if you're considering a slide, you will need up to 15 feet of deck space depending on the size of the slide. Check the standards of the NSPI for additional information.

THE SHELL THAT HOLDS THE WATER

Swimming pools can be completely or partially in-ground, anchored to hillsides, or placed directly on the surface of the ground. The type you select, as well as the availability of materials in your area, will determine the construction methods for your pool.

The majority of permanent pools are fully in-ground structures. They are the most accessible from patio areas and the most adaptable to unified landscape schemes. But both above-ground and partially in-ground pools can also be attractive and enjoyable.

The two most common types of pools are air-sprayed concrete—known as gunite or shotcrete—and vinyl-lined. Pools made of fiber-

glass are increasing in popularity.

You'll hear many conflicting claims about the merits of various types of pool construction, but beautiful and satisfactory pools can be made with each. The main thing is to have a knowledgeable contractor.

Concrete pools

Concrete is one of the most popular construction materials for swimming pools. Its workability, strength, permanence, and flexibility of design make it ideal for innovative and interesting in-ground and hillside pools.

The material is reinforced with steel rods to withstand the pressures of soil and water. The amount and size of the steel depends on the geographical location and the structural requirements.

The four main types of concrete construction are gunite, poured, hand-packed, and masonry block. Cost and availability of equipment usually determine which of these is used.

Several interior finishes are available in concrete pools. The surface may be plastered in colors ranging from white to black. Though white is still the most popular, dark colors are being used more and more because of their attractive appearance and a small solar heating benefit. Instead of plastering the concrete can be troweled smooth and painted in one of a variety of colors.

The most expensive finish is ceramic tile. Its appearance can be striking (see page 32) and it's easy to clean. Most owners compromise on a band of tile along the water line both for its attractiveness and for the ease of removing minerals, oil, and other dirt from it.

Gunite. This type of construction led the way to the growth in pool ownership because it was much cheaper than other methods of concrete construction (see page 86).

Gunite is a mixture of hydrated cement and sand applied over and under a grid of steel reinforcing rods—called rebar—directly against the soil. The mix is very dry and is shot from a nozzle under high pressure to form a one-piece shell that is considered stronger than any other type of concrete.

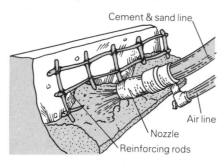

Cement & sand line

Air line

Nozzle

Reinforcing rods

The gunite must be directed behind the rebars and against the earth so that pockets of air or loose sand cannot form. The shell must be of the proper thickness through-

out, with no weak spots that will be unable to resist earth and hydrostatic pressures.

Many contractors place covers over the main drain pipe, inlet pipes, and light sockets to prevent their being filled with concrete. Otherwise, all openings must be checked and cleared as soon as the gunite crew is finished.

Gunite allows complete freedom of size and shape, since it follows any excavated shape. Steps and spas can be formed at the same time. The thickness of the shell and the number and size of the rebars can be adjusted to meet any structural requirement. If you have to build your pool on filled ground, a gunite shell supported on concrete piers that sit on solid ground may be the answer.

The initial cost of gunite equipment makes it impractical for the small contractor who builds only a few pools a year, unless the equipment can be rented when needed. If you don't live in a densely populated area, you may find either that gunite is not available or that the cost is considerably higher than other available materials.

Poured concrete. Largely replaced by gunite where the spray equipment is available, the poured concrete method has been abandoned by many companies because of the labor involved in setting the forms and the time it takes for the concrete to dry. After the

forms are stripped, the concrete floor is poured, spread, and then troweled smooth by hand.

The bond beam along the top of the wall is usually the last structural step, unless it is incorporated in the pour for the walls.

Steel reinforcing is used in this type of pool, too. The rebars projecting from the walls must be tied to the rebars in the floor and bond beam.

Unlike gunite, poured concrete limits your choice to simple rectangular and circular shapes.

Hand-packed concrete. This method has almost disappeared but may still be used in some rural areas.

Fewer forms are used than with a poured concrete pool, and much more hand labor is required. The same limitations on shape apply. The pool's sloping sides have two disadvantages—they make it more difficult for people to get out of the pool, and they don't lend themselves to competitive swimming.

Masonry blocks. Some small contractors favor this type of construction because there's a minimum outlay for equipment.

Because the blocks serve as forms and the cores are filled with mortar, a block pool is similar to a poured pool. There are two kinds of blocks—the most common are set in mortar; interlocking blocks,

TYPES OF POOL CONSTRUCTION

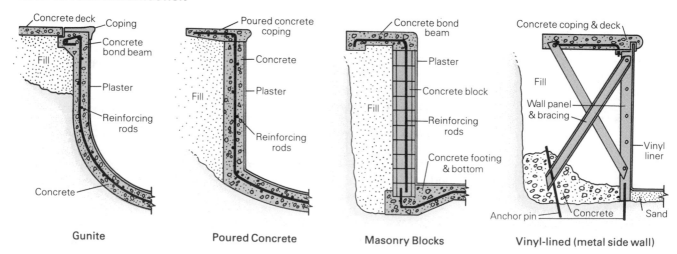

Gunite

Poured Concrete

Masonry Blocks

Vinyl-lined (metal side wall)

available in some areas, are easier to handle.

The blocks are stacked on a poured concrete footing. Reinforcing rods in the footing extend into the walls and floor. As the walls go up, openings must be left for plumbing and underwater lights.

The floor can be poured after the walls are up or at the same time the footing is poured. Steel is tied to rods projecting from the footing to form a solid grid. The floor is made with one pour and then troweled smooth.

The reinforcing rods projecting from the walls are bent down and wired to rods in the bond beam (see drawing on opposite page).

Because of the rectangular shape of the blocks, most pools of this type have straight lines—they are rectangular, wedge-shaped, L-shaped, or T-shaped. Curves can be incorporated into the design, but they should have not less than a 10-foot radius.

An interior finish must be applied to a masonry block pool to provide a waterproof surface for plaster and paint finishes.

Vinyl-lined pools

Even more than gunite, the development of vinyl-lined or vinyl pools has brought pool ownership within the budget of many people. The savings are greatest in the Northeast and Midwest, where these pools originated, because of the difficulty of building with concrete in a cold climate. Factory prefabrication from simple materials and short construction time—3 to 4 days is possible—make the difference (see page 86).

Sometimes, vinyl-lined pools are known as prepackaged pools because the builder only has to specify the size and shape desired. Within a few days, everything needed for a complete pool, including the support system and accessories, is delivered at one time.

The vinyl-lined pool is actually a large, flexible container supported on the sides by walls made of aluminum, steel, plastic, masonry block, or wood. The bottom of the liner rests on a bed of sand, vermiculite, or cement. The top of the liner is secured by a special coping that both gives a finished look to the edge of the pool and serves as a border for the deck. Divers can have a vinyl pool with a deep part either at one end or extending about two-thirds length of the pool.

Some sidewall structures are self-supporting, ideal for aboveground and on-ground installations. If used for in-ground pools, the pool can be filled with water before the excavation is backfilled.

The liner's lifetime is determined to a great extent by its environment and care. It is affected both by ultraviolet light from the sun and by pool alkalinity.

Fading due to ultraviolet light is prevented in some liners by the inclusion of ultraviolet inhibitors in the vinyl material. Some vinyls also have inhibitors that prevent staining by funguses in the sand underneath the liner. Chemicals do not affect it unless, by chance, chlorinated tablets are allowed to rest directly on the vinyl; chlorine is a bleach and can discolor the material. Because of its surface, the vinyl cleans easily and does not offer a home for algae.

Liners come in a range of colors and patterns. Rectangles and simple curved shapes are most popular, but special shapes can be made at a somewhat higher cost. Prefabricated steps and spas made from acrylic or fiberglass are available for vinyl-lined pools.

Aluminum sidewalls. For an aluminum shell, prefabricated panels are bolted together or extruded sections are interlocked with each other. The interlocking type allows for the design of freeform pools usually of specific shapes that fit prefabricated liners.

Steel sidewalls. Panels fabricated from galvanized steel are bolted together and supported by frames on the backside.

Plastic sidewalls. The use of molded plastic polymers for sidewall panels is relatively new. The panels are strong and lightweight, and do not corrode or deteriorate in

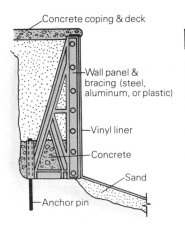

Vinyl-lined (plastic side wall)

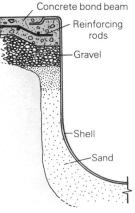

Fiberglass Shell

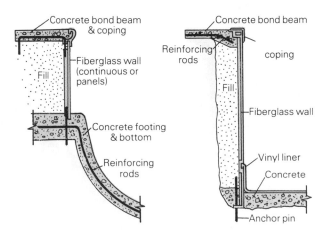

Hybrid Fiberglass   Low-hung Vinyl Liner

the ground. The material gives pool manufacturers an option against the increasing costs of steel and aluminum.

Masonry block sidewalls.
These are built in the same manner as described on page 18, except that they do not have to be leak-proof. The walls must be covered with smooth cement plaster to prevent tears and punctures in the liner, and they must be built to the exact size required by the prefabricated liner.

Wood sidewalls.
Advances made in recent years in pressure-treating wood to prevent rot and infestation make it possible to build a long-life wood shell for a vinyl-lined pool.

Fiberglass pools

In addition to the one-piece shell, there are several hybrids combining fiberglass sidewalls with bottoms of various materials.

The biggest advantage of fiberglass pools is low maintenance; the slick surface is difficult for algae to cling to and is easy to clean. Color is built right into the material, and usually no other surface finish is required. In areas where the alkaline content of the water is high, however, improperly maintained pool water can chalk the finish; the pool will then have to be painted.

Fiberglass shell.
Major improvements in the construction and installation of fiberglass shells have overcome the original problems of leaking, buckling, and adverse reaction to soil chemicals.

Since the size of the shells makes long distance transportation uneconomical, they may not be available outside of major population centers. As the demand increases however, more manufacturing plants are being established to extend the market for these pools.

The pool is constructed on an upside-down mold. To form the smooth surface on the inside of the pool, a layer of gelcoat containing the color is applied to the mold. Then, layers of resin-saturated fiberglass are laminated over the gelcoat to the desired thickness. Necessary reinforcement is added as the glass cloth is built up. The steps are built as part of the shell.

After the excavation is completed and the plumbing installed, a bed of sand is spread in the bottom of the hole and contoured to fit the shell. A crane picks the shell up off a trailer and swings it into place (right over the house, if necessary). After the plumbing is connected and the backfilling completed, the one-piece concrete bond beam and deck is poured integrally with the coping, which is part of the fiberglass shell (see also page 87).

The major disadvantage of the one-piece fiberglass mold is the limitation in size and shape. Since molds are massive and expensive, manufacturers offer only a few models.

Hybrid fiberglass.
These pools usually have 3-foot-high fiberglass sidewalls that may be made either from a continuous length or from flanged fiberglass sections bolted together with a leakproof seal. Some are designed to be installed with a concrete bottom and others with a vinyl bottom over sand—the latter type is called a "low-hung" vinyl-lined pool. The fiberglass is the same as in the one-piece shell.

The sidewalls are flexible and, in the case of a concrete-bottom pool, accommodate almost any size and shape. The low-hung pool's size and shape are limited by the capability of the liner manufacturer.

Portable pools

A popular alternative to a permanent pool is the portable, above-ground, vinyl-lined pool. More than 4 million of these are now in use.

Portable pools require no excavation, cost far less than a permanent pool, and are easily assembled and dismantled. For these reasons, people who don't want to make a big investment in swimming, families that want to try a pool first before making a commitment, and people who live in rented homes especially appreciate them.

Portable pools sit on the ground, and most have equal depth throughout (usually 4 feet). They may be circular (12 to 27 feet) in diameter), or rectangular or oval (12 by 18 feet to 18 by 39 feet).

Construction materials consist of self-supporting walls of galvanized steel or aluminum with interior vinyl liners. The bottom of the liner sits on a shallow bed of sand. The outer panels of the walls are often attractively colored and decorated.

You can choose a pool with or without decking. The decking can range from a sitting area on one side to one that surrounds the pool and is wide enough for patio furniture. The decks are railed for safety. Access to portable pools is by a ladder or steps supplied with the pool.

The height of the pool from the ground is a built-in safety feature—removal of the access ladder or steps effectively keeps small children from entering the pool.

Filter units, either sand, diatomaceous earth, or cartridge are specially designed for use with these pools. The skimmer generally is built in but may float on the surface. The support system, including filter, pump, skimmer, valves, and piping, is usually supplied as a package with the pool.

Installing a portable pool from a packaged kit can be a rewarding experience. Or, if you prefer, you can have the dealer install the pool. The portable pool can be dismantled and moved to a new location, an added attraction for mobile families. And because they're portable, most communities do not tax these pools as real property.

YOU CAN HAVE A SPA, TOO

Whether you're planning a pool or you already have one, you may want to contemplate the pleasures and benefits of therapeutic or hot water bathing.

Including a spa when you're building your pool is economically sound, especially when you build the spa integrally with a gunite, vinyl-lined, or hybrid fiberglass pool. Even installing a separate spa adjoining a pool can cost less than installing a spa by itself. You can use the same support system that heats and filters your pool water; piping, valves, and the fiberglass or gunite shell itself are additional expenses.

Concrete spas

These spas started as adjuncts to swimming pools, and that still is how most come into being.

Concrete's principal advantage is great durability coupled with the fairly easy maintenance of a hard cement finish. Concrete spas should have a ceramic tile ring at water level, since mineral scale forms there and is easier to remove from ceramic tile than from plaster.

Four methods can be used to build a concrete spa: gunite, masonry block, hand-packed concrete, and poured concrete. Gunite,

though requiring specialized equipment, is the most common method.

INTEGRAL CONCRETE SPA

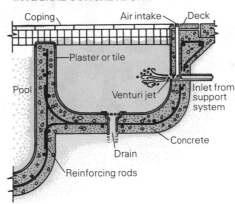

If you already have a concrete pool, you can add a concrete spa, but at significantly more expense than if spa and pool had been built at the same time. A portion of the pool wall must be broken out and the steel reinforcing rods for the new spa tied into the existing frame-work.

Fiberglass spas

Though gunite spas once were about the only residential type sold, fiberglass spas now proliferate in the marketplace. They are found in

every size, shape, and color imaginable. Most, though, are about 4 feet deep and 5 to 6 feet across.

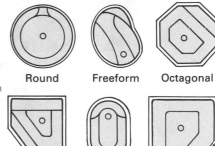

If you already own a swimming pool or are planning a pool that is not made of concrete, a fiberglass spa adjoining it and using the same support system is your most economical approach. And at least one manufacturer is offering a fiberglass shell that can be built in as part of your vinyl-lined pool when it is constructed.

Fiberglass spas are manufactured in the same way as fiberglass pools and enjoy the same characteristics, including easy maintenance.

TYPICAL FIBERGLASS SPA

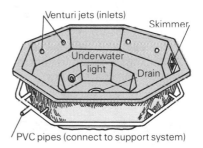

The lining. Most fiberglass shells have either an acrylic or gelcoat inner lining. The relative merits of acrylic versus gelcoat linings are the subject of some debate. Acrylic, a harder material, is more resistant to abrasion damage than is gelcoat. It also withstands chemical damage and high temperatures more readily.

Gelcoat performs well in all these departments, is less expensive, and is a good deal easier and less expensive to repair if time or accident should damage the finish.

INTEGRAL CONCRETE SPA SHAPES

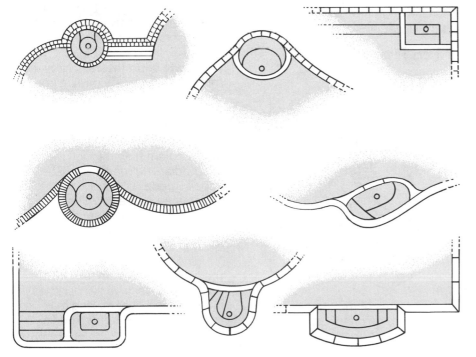

THE SUPPORT SYSTEM

For enjoyable swimming, you'll want a pool filled with comfortably warm, sparkling clear water that's free from harmful bacteria and other microorganisms and has the correct chemical balance.

It is the support system that heats, filters, and circulates the water to achieve the warmth and clarity you'll expect. In addition, the support system, as it circulates the water, evenly distributes the chemicals that you add to control purity and chemical balance.

THE FILTRATION SYSTEM

The filtration system, which recirculates and filters the water in the pool, is the only essential pool equipment. It enables you to use the initial water supply over and over again, adding just the little water necessary to backwash the filter and compensate for evaporation and splash-out.

The filtration system is composed of four elements: the filter, a pump and motor, an automatic surface skimmer, and recirculating piping. All the materials used should be corrosion resistant—certain types of stainless steel, bronze, plastic, or other nonferrous material.

The pump circulates the pool water through the filtration system, mixing the sanitizing chemicals and, if the water is heated, distributing the heated water evenly.

The water passes through the filter, which removes unwanted debris. The filter, along with chemical treatment (see page 100) and cleaning (see page 110), assures you of sparkling clear and sanitary water.

TYPICAL FILTER SYSTEM

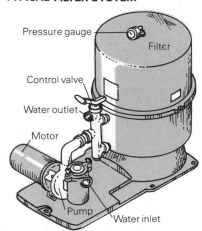

Pressure gauge
Filter
Control valve
Water outlet
Motor
Pump
Water inlet

The sizes of the various elements depend on the amount of water in the pool and the turnover time—the number of hours required for the system to filter the total amount of water; this varies from 8 to 12 hours, depending on usage. The more people using the pool at a given time, the faster the turnover time must be.

Which type of filter for you?

For residential pools there are three types of filters—high-rate sand, pressure diatomaceous earth (D.E.), and cartridge. Local code requirements will often determine the filter for your pool.

High-rate sand filters. Now the most popular for swimming pools, these filters are pressure vessels of fiberglass, stainless steel, or plastic with a system of drains and water distribution that maintains a nonturbulent flow through the filtering media. The media consist of special grades of sand, which, if maintained properly, will last for several years. Your filter supplier will recommend the proper sand for your unit.

The high-rate filter is based on the concept that high flow rates and pressures drive dirt particles into the sand bed, making maximum use of the filtering media.

Theoretically, if the filter were

POOL FILTERS

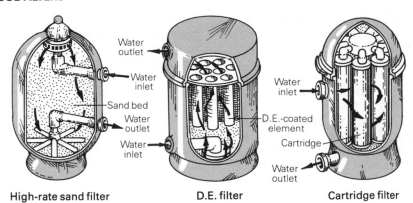

High-rate sand filter   D.E. filter   Cartridge filter

not backwashed, the dirt particles could reach the drain in the bottom and be returned to the pool. Actually, the pressure increase would stop the pump first. The pressure can be monitored on a gauge to determine when the filter should be backwashed.

Some 50 to 200 gallons of water, depending on the filter's size, is used during the backwash and must be disposed of. If your community prohibits the dumping of this water into the street, storm drains, or sewer line, you'll need a dry well to retain the water until it seeps into the ground.

Many manufacturers supply a complete filter, pump, and motor system pre-assembled and ready to connect to the recirculating piping and electrical supply.

Pressure diatomaceous earth (D.E.) filters. The next most popular after high-rate sand filters are D.E. filters, which offer the advantages of being more compact, filtering out smaller particles, and requiring less water for backwashing than the sand filters.

The D.E. filter strains water through diatomaceous earth, a sedimentary rock composed of microscopic fossil skeletons of the diatom, a small water animal. The skeletons have a highly porous structure of silica which makes them inert to most chemical action. The filtering is through a thin layer of D.E., which coats clothlike membranes or tubes. The D.E. rock is mined and then crushed, washed, sized, and packed as a white, chalky powder. The coarser sizes are more adaptable to pool filtration; the particular size best suited to your filter will be recommended by the manufacturer.

Disposing of the water after backwashing can be a problem if the use of sewers and storm drains is prohibited, as the D.E. will clog dry wells. Many D.E. filter systems come with separation tanks that hold about 75 gallons of the backwash water while the D.E. settles into a cloth filter. Then the water is returned to the pool and the D.E. is discarded. See page 100 for information on maintaining this type of filter.

Cartridge filters. Gaining quickly in popularity, the new cartridge filters are easy to remove and clean. Even though they must be replaced from time to time, the cost is low. A cartridge's life span is determined by the pool's use and environment. The more dirt that gets into your pool, the more often you'll have to replace the cartridge.

You'll need an extra set of cartridges for starting up a concrete pool. The residual plaster can be removed from the cartridges only by an acid wash. Most people will find it more convenient to throw them out and install new ones.

The major drawback of cartridge filters is that they do not consistently filter out the smaller particles.

Pump & motor

The combination of pump and motor draws water from the pool, forces it through the filter and heater, and returns it to the pool.

The pump is usually made of bronze or plastic and consists of the impeller (a bladed wheel),

FILTRATION SYSTEM SIZE

Pool Area Square Feet	Approximate Gallon Capacity	Cartridge Filters			High-Rate Sand Filters			Pressure D.E. Filters		
		Filter area	Gallons per min.	Pump H.P.	Filter area	Gallons per min.	Pump H.P.	Filter area	Gallons per min.	Pump H.P.
Less than 375	less than 15,000	45 sq. ft.	30	⅓–½	1.4 sq. ft.	25–30	½	15 sq. ft.	25–30	½
375 to 600	15,000 to 25,000	70 sq. ft.	50	½–¾	2.2 sq. ft.	30–45	¾	20–25 sq. ft.	35–50	½–¾
600 to 850	25,100 to 35,000	100 sq. ft.	75	¾–1	3.1 sq. ft.	45–60	¾–1	30–35 sq. ft.	55–70	¾–1
850 to 1100	35,100 to 45,000	135 sq. ft.	95	1–1½	4.9 sq. ft.	75–95	1–1½	35–40 sq. ft.	70–80	1–1½

Based on an average pool depth of 5.5 feet and a turnover of 8 hours.

The figures are for typical systems and may vary from manufacturer to manufacturer.

mounted on a shaft driven by the motor. Because of its rotational pumping action, it is known as a centrifugal pump.

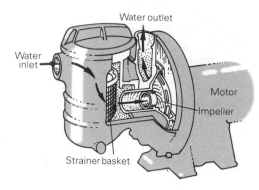

Most pool pumps are self-priming—that is, they expel all the air from the system when they start running and thus maintain a suction. Running a pump that has lost its prime will cause the pump to overheat and be damaged.

Self-priming pumps have a lint and hair filter on the intake side of the pump to catch large particles of foreign matter before they enter and clog the pump impeller.

When choosing a pump and motor, you'll want to consider the energy saving models. One way to compare the electrical efficiency of pumps is to compare the ratio of gallons pumped to kilowatt hours used. Just divide the gallons of water pumped in 1 hour by the pump rating in kilowatts. If the pump is rated in horsepower, convert the horsepower rating to kilowatts by multiplying it by 0.746. The higher the resulting number, the more efficient the pump.

Beware of claims emphasizing the horsepower of the pump; this is an incidental consideration if you expect to obtain the maximum operational economy. To determine the best pump size for a particular system, a professional support designer will do the following:

• Determine the total number of gallons in the pool (see page 27).
• Select ther proper turnover rate for the pool.
• Calculate the needed pipe sizes for minimal friction losses.
• Calculate the total head

(pressure) and flow requirements of the pool system.
• From the pump performance curves, select the pump that meets the calculated requirements. The performance curve of a pump indicates the number of gallons per minute it can pump against a range of pressure heads.
• Choose a filter model which will accept the number of gallons per minute that the selected pump is rated for at the total head of the system. Follow the manufacturer's guidelines for the filter media selected.
• Choose electrical wiring and circuit breaker sizes recommended in the pump installation manual.
• Consider the use of time clocks that precisely control the periods that pump and heater are on.

Points to consider when choosing a pump are its pumping capacity relative to your pool size, the pump's operating costs, and maintenance needs. To avoid corrosion, as many parts as possible should be made of materials that are corrosion resistant. The motor should be water resistant, and electrically isolated and insulated.

Installing the pump requires some care. It should be at or slightly above water level and as close to the pool as possible. If it's located more than 40 feet from the pool, the piping diameter must be increased to overcome the additional head loss.

The surface skimmer

In a properly designed pool circulating system, one or more surface skimmers connected to the pump intake pull dirt, oils, lotions, floating algae, and leaves into the filtration system. Suction from the main drain outlet at the deepest point in the pool will not pull these materials down, as they collect on the surface of the water.

Most skimmers are built into the pool, though units that hang on the side of the pool are also available for portable or in-ground pools built without skimmers.

Several varieties of built-in skimmers are made. Most are de-

signed with a filter basket to remove large debris. You can also purchase a unit with a built-in filter cartridge, a sensing device that automatically replaces lost water, or an automatic dispenser for chlorination. A vacuum or suction connection may be part of the skimmer, for use when vacuuming the pool.

The usual surface skimmer is made of precast concrete or plastic and consists of a tank with a projecting throat on its upper side. A self-adjusting floating weir performs the skimming action by regulating the amount of water that enters the skimmer. Because it adjusts to allow only a thin sheet of water to spill over, velocity and not volume is the key to good skimming.

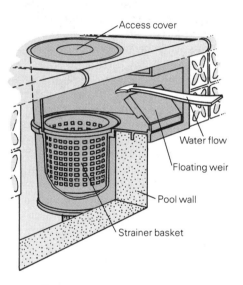

The skimmer will be most effective when it is located on the down-wind side of the pool; the wind helps the pump by pushing debris toward the opening.

Piping the system

The plumbing system is designed to circulate all the water from the pool through the filtration system. Normally, water is drawn from the pool through the main drain and the surface skimmer; passes through suction lines to the pump, filter, and heater; and then returns to the pool via return lines.

The main outlet or drain is a precast concrete or plastic sump,

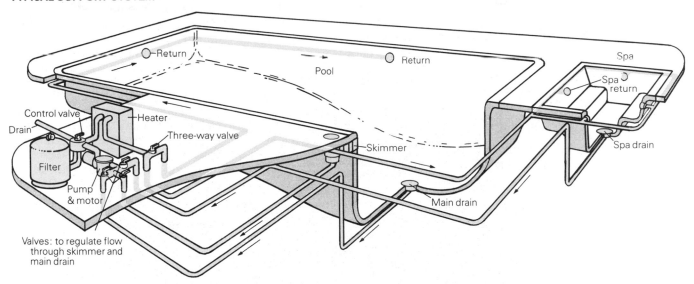

either covered with a grill or designed with an antivortex feature to lessen the chance of a child being trapped by the suction.

Located in the deepest part of the pool, the main drain serves as a collecting point for debris and draws off dirt that settles in the bottom. It also allows for complete draining of the pool. Another intake can be the vacuum line for the cleaner, though in most pools this connection is part of the skimmer.

Suction and return lines must be of adequate size if the filter system is to work properly (see chart on page 23). The number and location of the return lines and inlets required for proper circulation of the water in the pool depend on the pool's size and shape. Swivel fittings at the ends of the return lines allow the water flow to be directed for good circulation and direct the surface water toward the skimmers. Proper circulation is essential for complete filtration of the pool water and for thorough mixing of the chemicals.

In the Northern Hemisphere, the arrangement should encourage a clockwise movement in the pool water. In pools of complex shape, the inlets should be located so that there are no dead spots. It's desirable to maintain equal flows through the inlets. This can be done by progressively reducing the pipe size of the return line between one inlet and the next.

Though copper pipe is acceptable, most pool builders use one of several types of plastic for piping and fittings. Plastics' low cost, complete resistance to corrosion, good flow characteristics, flexibility, and ease of installation make it practical for all pool piping. The plastics are joined with a solvent welding compound and the flexible types can be formed easily without kinking.

Some local building codes have not yet accepted plastic pipe; most that do specify the plastic types and wall thicknesses they allow. Be sure to check the codes in your area.

Some types of automatic pool cleaners require piping that is built into the pool wall or installed while the pool is being built. Decide what cleaner you will use before you build your pool (see page 89).

Hooking up the spa

If you've decided on a spa as part of your pool, or if you've located one close by, you can use the pool support system for the spa. The drawing above shows how the spa can be integrated into the pool system. If your pool relies on solar heat, you'll want a gas heater for the spa.

Activating the water. The basic mover of water in a spa is the pool pump. To give a real sensation of moving water, the pump is boosted with either venturi jets or a blower, and sometimes both.

A venturi jet, also called hydro jet, restricts the flow of water in a tube, thereby increasing its velocity.

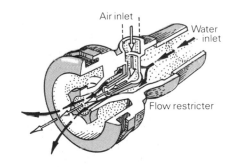

Venturis can be fixed units or can have a swivelling eyeball to allow changing the direction of the flow. Some have a separate air intake to produce bubbles.

Blowers produce more intense bubble action than a venturi alone by introducing air into the venturi, or blowing air through separate inlets. They are usually controlled by their own switch so bubbles can be options.

These blowers must be at least 12 inches above water level or must be protected from flooding by air loops and check valves.

HEATING THE POOL

Is it worth the considerable additional expense to heat a pool? After weighing all the pros and cons, you will probably find that it is.

Most people feel comfortable in water that's 78°F/26°C to 80°F/27°C. Though you may find an air temperature of 70°F/21°C enjoyable, you'd feel chilly in a pool at the same temperature.

An unheated pool does store heat from the sun, but it will never exceed the average air temperature. Unless you live in a very warm climate, you won't have much swimming in that comfortable 80°F/27°C water if you don't heat your pool. A heater will allow you to swim for more months of the year and more hours each day—and even evenings, too.

Comparing the added expenses of a heater—equipment cost and installation, annual maintenance by an expert, and, of course, escalating fuel costs—to your large investment in the pool and the additional use you'll make of your investment will help you decide.

You can heat your pool with gas, electricity, or oil, or you can let the sun do it for you. In the next chapter, ''The Solar-heated Pool,'' beginning on page 29, you'll read about ways to take advantage of solar energy to heat your pool. In sunnier parts of the United States, the sun may be all you need.

In other parts of the country, though, solar heating may not be practical, or you may have to supplement it with a traditional fuel.

Gas is the most common and usually the cheapest and most efficient heating fuel. Though natural gas shortages have been widely predicted, most experts now seem to agree that there is plenty of gas available at the right price. Sometimes, pool users find themselves a target of natural gas conservation efforts, but as a whole, they are insignificant consumers. In some parts of the country, natural gas use is being encouraged.

In the face of high fuel costs, you'll hear many conflicting claims about the most cost-effective way to heat a pool. A recent study provides some helpful information. The single most effective way to lower your heating costs is to cover your pool when it's not being used. The cover prevents heat loss during the night and allows the sun to heat the water during the day (see pages 30, 53, and 65).

Even with a solar cover, you'll need supplemental heat—oil, electric, or solar—in many parts of the country. On a 10-year basis, including all equipment and operating costs, the study concluded that a gas heater and solar cover combination was a third to one half the cost of any other option. Of course, a change in utility rates or less than maximum use of the cover can invalidate the conclusions. So check for yourself in your area and compare your options.

Types of heaters

There are three main types of pool heaters. Open-flame fired with gas or oil and electric heaters are discussed here. Solar heating is covered in the next chapter, which begins on page 29.

Open-flame. The most commonly used, open-flame heaters are available for any size residential pool. Because gas heaters are the most popular, manufacturers have developed high-efficiency gas heaters for pool use. Advances in the design of the heat exchanger (through which the pool water passes) and the combustion chamber, as well as the use of electric pilots and narrow range ther-

POOL HEATER SIZE					
Pool Area (square feet)	BTU/hr Input At Average Temperature Difference—Coldest Month*				
	10°F	15°F	20°F	25°F	30°F
200	30,000	45,000	60,000	75,000	90,000
300	45,000	67,500	90,000	112,500	135,000
400	60,000	90,000	120,000	150,000	180,000
500	75,000	112,500	150,000	187,500	225,000
600	90,000	135,000	180,000	225,000	270,000
700	105,000	157,500	210,000	262,500	315,000
800	120,000	180,000	240,000	300,000	360,000
900	135,000	202,500	270,000	337,500	405,000
1000	150,000	225,000	300,000	375,000	450,000

*Average temperature difference is found by subtracting the mean temperature of the coldest month the pool is to be used (obtain from Weather Bureau) from the desired pool temperature.

The chart is for oil or natural gas heaters at sea level and is based on the formula: POOL AREA (square feet) × 15 × TEMPERATURE DIFFERENCE (°F).

Table based on 80 percent heater efficiency

For electric heaters, multiply BTUs/hr by 0.8

Correction for elevation—add 4 percent to computed pool area for each 1000 feet above sea level.

Above-ground pools and pools in windy areas will require larger heaters. Pools in enclosures can use smaller heaters.

POOL HEATERS

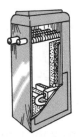

Coil heater
(oil or gas)

Tank heater
(oil or gas)

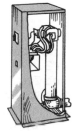

Convection heater
(oil or gas)

Electric heater

mostats, have increased heater efficiency by about 15 percent.

You will find three variations of open-flame heaters—coil, tank, and convection.

Coil heaters, also known as flash heaters, present a small, fast-moving volume of water to a large flame. They work very fast and can be used in any size pool.

Tank heaters, similar to your home hot-water heater, present a large volume of slow-moving water to a small flame. They have long recovery periods and are not very efficient in cold climates, but they are less expensive than coil heaters. Their use is limited to small pools and spas.

Convection heaters are a hybrid of the other two and sometimes incorporate a booster pump. They use a large flame to heat slow-moving water. Relatively inexpensive, they're limited to small pools and spas.

Electric heaters. Models that have electric heating elements immersed in the water work slowly, so they're practical only for spas.

Another type of electric heater works on the heat-pump principle, using refrigerant, heat exchangers, and a compressor to transfer heat

from the air to the pool water. Units are expensive; whether they're economical to operate depends on energy costs and climate in your area.

What size heater?

The sizes of gas and oil heaters are indicated in British Thermal Units (BTUs). A BTU is the amount of heat required to raise the temperature of one pound of water one degree Fahrenheit. Most of the heat loss from a pool is from the surface; it takes about 12 to 15 BTUs an hour to raise the temperature of a square foot of pool surface water that much.

You can calculate the number of BTUs required to heat your pool. First you need to know the mean temperature of the coldest month in which you'll use it, the temperature you want the water to be, and either the surface area of the pool or the number of gallons that it holds. Then factor in the heater efficiency to arrive at the BTU/hour input to the heater. This is the way that all heaters except electric ones are rated. Electric heaters are rated in kilowatts input, one kilowatt equaling 3412 BTUs.

To estimate heater size, calculate the surface area of your pool as shown at right, and then, from the table on the facing page, find the heater size you'll need for the temperature difference required. Windy sites and other climate considerations will affect this approximate value. If your pool is enclosed or has a cover, fewer BTUs are required. Remember that an undersized heater will increase the cost of heating your pool.

In areas where competition is strong among pool builders, you can end up with a heater that's too small for your pool. A builder anxious to close a sale can make a bid more competitive by selecting a marginally sized heater. If it's too small to heat the pool properly and efficiently, you may have to replace it later.

You'll avoid this possibility if you select your pool builder with care and make your own estimate of heater size.

ESTIMATING POOL AREA AND VOLUME

Areas in square feet of surface
Volumes in gallons of water

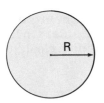

Area = R x R x 3.14
Volume = area x average depth x 7.5

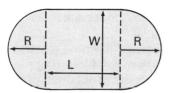

Area = (A + B) x L x 0.45 (approx.)
Volume = area x average depth x 7.5

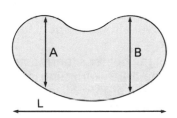

Area = (L x W) + (R x R x 3.14)
Volume = area x average depth x 7.5

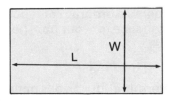

Area = L x W
Volume = area x average depth x 7.5

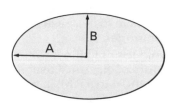

Area = A x B x 3.14
Volume = area x average depth x 7.5

ENERGY-SAVING SUGGESTIONS

As energy costs skyrocket, keeping your pool maintenance and operating expenses within your budget will become more and more challenging. Here are some ideas to help you reduce the costs of heating, filtering, cleaning, and treating your pool water.

Heating the Pool

• Use a pool cover or blanket, the single best water and fossil fuel conservation device, and have it in place when the pool is not in use. The cover will reduce heating bills by preventing heat loss, save on chemicals, and reduce water evaporation. A solar cover allows the pool to collect heat from the sun.

• Set the heater's thermostat to 78° F/ 26° C, the most healthful swimming temperature, or below. An increase of 1° F will increase your use of natural gas by 10 percent.

• Use an accurate thermometer to measure pool water temperature. When it reaches the desired level, mark the proper setting on the thermostat and allow no further adjustments. If your pool is not used at all during the week, you can reduce the thermostat setting 8 to 10 degrees during the week, moving it back to its proper setting for the weekend.

• Set the filter time clock to start the pump no earlier than 6 A.M. during the pool heating season. It's at this time that the nightly heat loss stabilizes.

• During extended periods when the pool is not in use, shut off the heater and pilot light.

• Shelter the pool from the wind with wind breaks—shrubs and other plantings, fences, or pool buildings.

• Follow a program of regular preventive maintenance for your pool heater (see page 100).

Filtering the Pool

To determine your pool's optimum filtration time, gradually reduce the filtering time in half hour steps until water clarity and chemical balance begin to deteriorate; then increase the time in half hour increments until the water regains its clarity chemical balance. This can reduce electrical consumption by 40 to 50 percent. For periods of heavy pool use, you may have to increase the filtering time to 8 hours or longer.

• Avoid running the filtration system during the peak hours of electrical usage, noon to 6 P.M. in summer and 4 to 9 P.M. in winter. The best time to operate the filtration system is between 6 A.M. and noon.

• For maximum efficiency, follow a program of regular preventive maintenance for the pump and filter (see page 100). Remove foreign material regularly from the strainer baskets in the pump and skimmer.

• When the pool is in heavy use, turn on the filter manually, returning it to automatic operation after the swimmers have left the pool.

Cleaning the Pool

• If you have an automatic pool cleaner with its own pump, operate it for 3 to 4 hours a day during the swimming season and 2 to 3 hours a day during the off-season. If this doesn't adequately clean the pool or if there's an abnormal amount of dirt entering the pool, increase the cleaning time by half hour increments until adequate cleaning is accomplished.

• Use your leaf skimmer and wall brush regularly and frequently.

Saving Pool Water

• Turn off the tile spray device on your automatic pool cleaner—much of the water evaporates before it even hits the tile and scale formation will be reduced.

• Prevent splashout by plugging in the overflow line when the pool is in use.

• Reevaluate your backwashing schedule, particularly if your filter doesn't have a separation tank (see page 23). Backwashing too often wastes water.

Conserving Pool Chemicals

• Add chlorine during the evening hours whenever possible. If you have a feeder that uses pellets or cakes, you may have to supplement the chlorine feeding by hand.

• Keep pool water chemistry in balance and check it regularly (see page 101). Maintain pool water pH between 7.4 and 7.6.

• Keep the water conditioned to reduce chemical consumption (see page 104). Maintain a minimum of 30 ppm of cyanuric acid.

• Trim back excess foliage around the pool and keep the deck areas clean to reduce chemical cleaning and filtering needs.

THE SOLAR-HEATED POOL

For several reasons, solar heating and swimming pools are an exceedingly compatible combination. First, the cost of conventional heat is so high (simply because the pool loses so much heat from its broad, exposed surface every night and every cloudy day) that it makes solar costs look very inviting.

Second, the swimming season corresponds to the months of high, hot sun and long days, when plenty of solar heat is available.

And finally, because pools don't need large amounts of high-intensity heat, and because they act as their own heat-transfer liquid and heat storage, heating a pool requires only a few uncomplicated pieces of equipment.

Pools can be heated by the sun and the heat retained in several different ways—by positioning the pool to take the best advantage of the sun, by protecting the pool from the wind, by enclosing or covering it, and by using a solar water heating system.

A PLACE IN THE SUN

Locating the pool where it can receive the maximum number of hours of sunlight possible is the first step in solar heating your pool. For more on this, see "Choosing a Pool Site," page 6. If your pool has its proper place in the sun, the sun will heat the water directly; then, if you want, you can increase the heating effect by using a solar blanket, embedding water heating coils in the deck, and incorporating a dark bottom in your pool.

WIND...THE HEAT THIEF

While the sun and a heater are pumping heat into your pool, the wind sets up convection currents that steal that same heat at an alarming rate. Every square foot of the pool's surface gives up heat to the wind by evaporation, and the stronger the wind, the greater the heat loss. Evaporation alone accounts for 60 percent of the heat loss from the pool. Another 30 percent of the loss radiates into the air from the water surface and 10 percent goes into the ground.

To minimize the wind's effects, you can locate the pool where it's protected from the wind (see page 8), erect screens or fences (see page 90), and enclose or cover the pool.

HOW A POOL LOSES HEAT

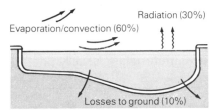

Radiation (30%)
Evaporation/convection (60%)
Losses to ground (10%)

Pool enclosures

Depending on the climate in your area, swimming in an outdoor pool can be uncomfortable during spring and fall, even if the pool is heated, and almost impossible in winter. An enclosed pool may allow you to extend your swimming season. You can either purchase one of the manufactured canopies, extend your house to include a "pool room," or improvise an enclosure to fit the pool and its surroundings. You can even have an inside-outside pool (see page 57).

In addition to permitting year-round use, the enclosures will control summer winds, enable you to do more night swimming, lower heating costs, and keep out most insects and debris.

Having a roof over your pool allows moisture to condense, creating "greenhouse" conditions. When the temperature outside begins to drop, a completely closed room can become excessively humid and uncomfortable. In designing an enclosure or including a pool as an extension of the house, be sure to plan for maximum ventilation to control humidity.

A variety of manufactured pool enclosures are available. The most economical are air-inflated canopies, one of which doubles as a pool cover when deflated. These structures are held down either by a rim of water that serves as an anchor or by fasteners in the deck. A blower provides the slight pressure necessary to keep the canopy inflated. If the canopy is ever punc-, tured or torn, the constant injection of air should prevent it from collapsing suddenly and cause it instead to settle slowly to the surface.

Another type of enclosure is constructed of lightweight metal frames paneled with opaque, translucent, or clear fiberglass-reinforced plastic. Some of these enclosures are constructed with roll-back roof and/or side panels to allow summer ventilation. Most manufacturers recommend a minimum of 3 or 4 feet of enclosed deck area around the water.

Other more permanent enclosures of wood, or masonry combined with wood, are also available, but at higher costs.

Extending your house lines to accommodate a pool is usually the most expensive method of sheltering the area. Costs will depend on your location and the type of wall and roof coverings you use.

Be sure to check building codes before investing in a pool enclosure. Some cities consider them accessory buildings (the inflated canopy type included), which means they are subject to setback laws, land development ordinances, and load requirements.

Pool covers

Depending on material and design, a cover serves several purposes.
• Any cover prevents heat loss by evaporation and radiation. According to the National Spa and Pool Institute, a cover will keep the pool 10° to 15°F warmer than if it were not covered.
• A solar cover or blanket can allow the pool to collect heat from the sun.
• A safety cover can prevent children or animals from falling into the pool.
• By helping to keep the pool clean and free from leaves and other debris, particularly during the winter months when the pool is not used, it can reduce the amount of time and electricity needed to operate the pump and filter system.

Caution must be exercised when using a pool cover. Covers must be removed **completely** when the pool is in use, especially if the cover floats on the surface. A child or even an adult surfacing under a cover may not be able to lift it sufficiently to get air. Suffocations and drownings have been caused by pool covers only partially removed.

Pool covers come in a variety of styles. Some are rigid and are lifted mechanically to form a canopy (see page 53); others are flexible and can be removed manually or stored on a roller (hand or motor-driven); still others are made in sections that float on the pool.

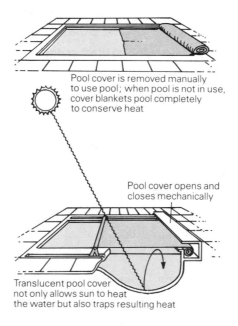

Pool cover is removed manually to use pool; when pool is not in use, cover blankets pool completely to conserve heat

Pool cover opens and closes mechanically

Translucent pool cover not only allows sun to heat the water but also traps resulting heat

Cover materials. Usually, pool covers are made from different forms of plastic—sheet, foam, bubble, or mesh. The rigid cover on page 53 is corrugated fiberglass panels mounted on aluminum frames.

Plastic sheet can be clear, translucent, or opaque black. All prevent heat loss by convection and radiation. Transparent and translucent materials allow the sun's rays to heat the pool water.

Plastic sheet must be anchored to the deck; it can be folded or rolled up for storage.

Winterizing covers are often made from heavy-gauge plastic sheet.

Foam for pool covers takes either one of two forms—it may be large foam slabs, or blanket sandwiched between two pieces of plastic sheet. Both the slabs and the blanket float on the waves and are more efficient than plastic sheet in reducing heat loss.

The slabs are the more efficient insulators—their insulating qualities increase with their thickness. But the thicker they are, the more they diminish the heating effect of the sun on the water. It's a case of good news and bad—they keep warm water warm, but they also keep chilly water chilly.

A blanket can be rolled up or folded, but the foam slabs must be fished from the pool and stacked. Sometimes 1 or more inches thick, the slabs require considerable labor to install and remove; space must also be provided to store them.

Bubble plastic covers float on the water's surface. They not only prevent heat loss by evaporation and radiation, but also allow the sun to heat the water. A bubble plastic blanket can be folded or rolled up for storage.

Mesh covers made from woven plastic fibers prevent some heat loss, but are best used for safety purposes and winterizing.

SOLAR HEATERS

Solar pool heating has the advantage of economy—homeowners turn to it because gas or electric pool heaters cost so much to run that they threaten to become unaffordable. A solar pool heating system, on the other hand, is virtually free once the saving in fuel costs equals the cost of the solar equipment and installation.

Unlike solar heating for a home, solar pool heating is remarkably adaptable. Its low operating temperatures (100°F/82°C) and summer use free it somewhat from the more stringent requirements of solar heating a home. The relatively high summer sun—from June through September—is readily available, and even a fairly low efficiency of solar collection is enough to provide all the heat a pool needs.

As a result of this design flexibility, there are successful solar pool heating systems in which the collectors crop up in all kinds of unusual situations: on fences, poolhouse roofs, banks and hillsides, and garage roofs. Some even face directions other than directly south.

Collectors in the form of water heating coils can even be embedded in a dark concrete deck surrounding the pool (see page 52). This method will work only if the pool receives full sun. One advantage is that the sometimes unsightly collectors are concealed; also, the water circulating in the coils absorbs heat from the deck's surface and reduces its temperature to a comfortable level. If installing this system, be sure that the contractor has experience in building this type of collector. Improper installation can cause the concrete to crack.

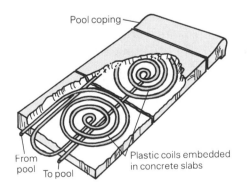

Pool coping

From pool   To pool

Plastic coils embedded in concrete slabs

To heat the pool, a pump cycles pool water through the solar collec-

tors and back to the pool again (see below). A differential thermostat turns on the pump when the collectors are hot enough to benefit the pool. Most systems also include a regular pool filter and an auxiliary heater.

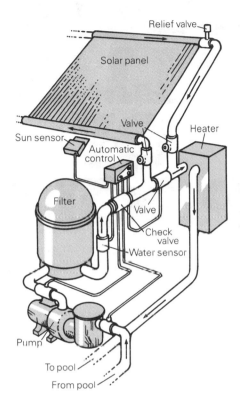

Relief valve

Solar panel

Valve

Sun sensor   Heater

Automatic control

Filter

Valve

Check valve

Water sensor

Pump

To pool

From pool

The most common pool collectors are extruded from plastic polymers which, in quality collectors, are stabilized against the life-shortening effects of heat and ultraviolet rays from the sun. The inert plastic cannot be corroded by pool chemicals or eroded by the fast-moving water; and it does not allow scale to build up in the water passages.

The black color, essential for efficient heating, is permanent, unlike metal collectors which must be painted every few years. Prices of quality stabilized polymer panels are comparable to the best metal collectors.

The simplest, least efficient, and shortest-lived collectors are made from coils of black plastic tubing. The type of plastic used is not resistant to ultraviolet.

Metal collectors, most common for domestic water heating, may be used as pool heaters. The metal passages can be corroded by pool chemicals and eroded by high water flow rates, causing leaks. Scale deposits can clog the water passages and reduce water flow. For best heating efficiency, the metal must be blackened, usually with paint. Prices vary widely.

A solar pool heater can extend your swimming season by 2 to 4 months, depending on your geographical location. In California, a season can run from April to October; in New England, it's more likely to last from June to September.

Choosing a solar heating contractor

It's best to deal with a company that has its own design and installation staff and service organization. Their experience in servicing their own systems, particularly when under warranty, usually spurs improvements in the next installations. The major manufacturers train their distributors' staffs in the design, installation, and servicing of their systems.

Be sure to compare warranties and obtain copies and have a written understanding of where the manufacturer's responsibility ends and the contractor's begins. Also ask for an owner's manual or operating and service instructions.

Information on contracts and contractors begins on page 82.

THE DARK-BOTTOMED POOL

Usually, pools are plastered in black or dark green or painted in dark colors for esthetic reasons—such pools look like lakes or ponds, reflecting nearby trees and shrubs. Take a look at one, though, before deciding on a dark-bottomed pool. If these dark pools are located in the sun, they benefit from slightly increased solar heating; the gain, though, is difficult to measure.

A COLOR GALLERY OF POOLS

Kersplash! That first wet thrill of summer as you cascade into the sparkling deep may be the premium pleasure of having a pool at home. But other bonuses are plentiful, too—solitary laps down its length before breakfast, splash-happy afternoons for the kids, fast rounds of water volleyball, exhilarating dips after soaks in spa or hot tub, and relaxed poolside lingering with family and friends on warm summer evenings.

In hot weather, the most immediate promise of pleasure may be to plunge right in. But with attention to landscaping detail, a swimming pool becomes more than just a source of water play, exercise, or relaxation in an adjoining spa. The quietly lapping and sparkling presence of a swimming pool is pleasant to look at and refreshing to live with throughout the year.

In the upcoming pages you'll see pools not just in the typical backyard site but in all kinds of locations—pools set alongside houses and even in front of them, on rises above houses and in vales below, on small city lots as well as in open, spacious gardens. As you browse through these pages, keep watch for ideas that may apply to your situation. In every example, notice how pools can interplay with plantings, pavings, decks, fences, and other structures to create a unified landscaping scheme.

So you can better visualize some of these landscape designs, we've included drawings; the ▶ on each drawing indicates the position of our camera when the accompanying photograph was taken.

Though sunshine and swimming have always been natural partners, they're more closely linked now than ever before. Most of the pools in these photographs have some form of solar heating or some other energy-saving feature. You're sure to discover something new here that will guide you if you decide to try the solar approach.

Surprise! Making waves with a colossal splash, diver delights onlookers soaking in adjacent spa. Dark tiles on bottom and sides give pool its distinctive deep blue color. Design: Chris Benson and Gianni Siracusa.

THE BACK YARD PLUNGE

Starkly simple but very elegant, this design uses brick for pavement, coping, and stepped plant ledge at far end of pool. Bowed shape of pool mirrors curves of boxwood hedges. Design: Tom Baak.

Back yard swimming hole with naturalistic setting creates Huck Finn scene—rope-encircled wooden pilings line pierlike deck, ivy dangles over rocks, and trickling waterfalls circulate water. Design: George Meyer.

...back yard plunge

Popular vinyl-lined pool transforms yard into recreation and entertainment center. Slide and diving board provide hours of fun. Wooden deck connects back of house to pool area. Design: Leisuretime Pools.

Desert oasis blends linear form of pool and raised deck with rounded boulders and bushy desert plantings. Concealed pump sends water cascading over boulder into pool. Design: Guy Greene.

Small is beautiful—and saves space and energy, as well—in this shallow (4½ feet deep) and under-sized (18 feet in diameter) pool with attached spa. Shape of pool is echoed in graceful lines of intimate seating area. Design: Bill Kapranos.

What goes up can come down: with some work, above-ground pool that's 4 feet deep can go up in spring and fold down in autumn, or it can be kept up all year. Design: National Pool Builders.

...back yard plunge

Up among the trees on a sloping site, above-ground pool with wooden deck overhanging rim looks like an in-ground installation. Unheated pool offers an invigorating dip after a soak in solar-heated fiberglass spa on raised patio.

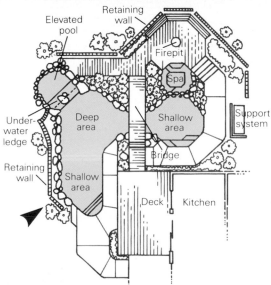

Elevated pool

Retaining wall

Firepit

Spa

Underwater ledge

Deep area

Shallow area

Support system

Retaining wall

Shallow area

Bridge

Deck

Kitchen

Tropical paradise in your back yard? This freeform pool with its many special features is a fantasy-come-true. Swimmers can savor waterfall from underwater ledge, or cross a bridge to raised deck, spa, and firepit. Set at bottom of a slope, pool wraps around one side of house; a retaining wall of railroad ties tames hill. Rocks partially embedded in concrete surround much of pool and catch trickles from spa. Design: John Withers, Master Pools by Geremia.

PUTTING THE POOL OUT IN FRONT

Stunningly contemporary, front yard pool and patio combination turns long and narrow lot into inviting entertainment area. Design preserves part of front lawn; potted plants add poolside color. Vine-covered fence separates entry walkway on far side from pool area. Design: Robert Royston, Royston, Hanamoto, Alley & Abey.

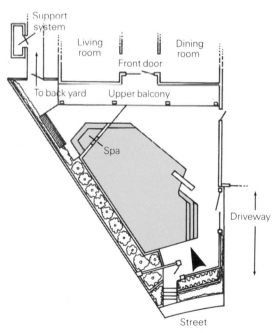

Shoehorned into a wedge-shaped lot, pool and spa take advantage of available front yard space, leaving back yard as private family area. Geometric pool meets challenge of lot and still leaves room for walkway on one side. Entire area can be brightly lighted at night for safety. Front entry wall and gate are staggered to block view from street (see drawing). Design: Fred Fritsinger.

THE URBAN POOL

Tucked into a small urban lot, above-ground pool and deck are easily accessible from spacious living room behind. Solar collectors out of sight on roof heat pool the year around. Design: Larry Wilson.

Startlingly lush hideaway in an urban setting, round above-ground pool and its plantings make careful use of space. Deck flows from house to rim of pool in this compact design. Design: Larry Wilson.

Raised planting area

Street

Hand holds

Storage room

Sculpture

Covered patio

Entry

Den

Tunnel sculpture—a painted and waxed concrete slab —dramatically divides urban pool into two parts and makes it seem larger than it is. From house (view above), small circular pool beyond tunnel is mostly concealed, hinting at an expanse that does not exist. Circular pool is shallow; hand holds set into concrete sides provide extra margin of safety. Design: Rod Garrett.

BUILDING ON CHALLENGING SITES

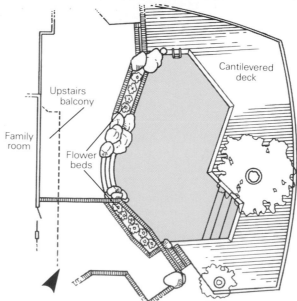

Cliff-hanging pool perched high on a steep, wooded hillside is anchored securely to piers sunk 30 feet below ground. Cedar deck cantilevers out from edge of pool; pool equipment is concealed below deck. Design: Richard Murray. Pool: Peri-Bilt Pools.

Cantilevered deck

Upstairs balcony

Family room

Flower beds

Double challenge—steep site and lack of access for standard excavating equipment—made pool difficult to build. A small tractor notched pool site into hillside; excavated dirt was used to extend grassy area below pool. Design: John Shelton.

Seemingly suspended off edge of cliff, keyhole-shaped pool reaches out across canyon. Low but deep wall surrounding much of pool permits unobstructed view. Circle of keyhole is diving area; cabana at opposite end contains a shower and changing area. Design: Paul Sterling Hoag.

Challenging Sites **45**

...challenging sites

Notched into a small, steep site, pool meanders through woods, adding space for outdoor living where none had existed before. Gunite pool wall faced with flagstone extends above water line to contain hill. Design: Rod Garrett.

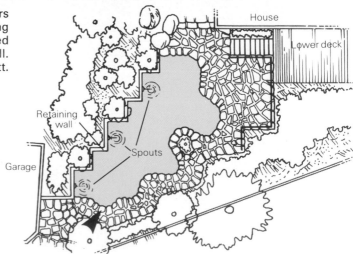

House

Lower deck

Retaining wall

Spouts

Garage

Sylvan retreat in compact space...
pool uses evergreens, flowing
waterfall, and boulders to create
natural-looking environment. Deck
at side of pool is slightly tilted to
direct water into a central drain.
Design: John Withers, Master Pools
by Geremia. Waterfall: Zierden
Waterfalls.

Shallow side yard lap pool with
attached spa puts found space
to good use. Gently curving sides
edged with uneven slabs keep pool
from looking too linear in long, narrow space. Design: Don Burgess.

FROM WINE TO WATER: RECYCLED POOLS

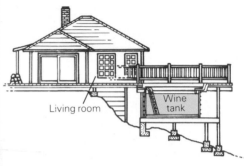

Living room

Wine tank

Unheated plunge pool—originally a 12-foot-diameter wine tank—now serves as focus for entertaining on this intimate hillside deck. Octagonal cedar bench encircles pool and provides two levels of built-in seating. Design: Wagstaff & McDonald.

Like a plunge into mulled wine, swimming in this tank was affected at first by wine sediment leaching into water. Water cleared when filter and pump were added. Deck by pool does double duty as carport. Used wine tanks, like those shown on these pages, are sometimes available from wineries. In some areas you can buy a new one—look under "Tanks" in the Yellow Pages. Design: Gary Patterson.

For splashing good fun and a cooling dip on a hot summer day, huge converted wine tank makes perfect play pool.

HARNESSING THE SUN: SOLAR HEATING

Sunny solution—their house lacked a roof with southern exposure, so owners built poolside cabana on an open site facing south and installed solar panels on its roof to take full advantage of all-day sun. Cabana contains ample room for changing and pool equipment storage. Design: David Steiner, Philip Grimes, Bob Cornfield.

Hidden from house behind retaining wall and deck rail, two tiers of glazed solar panels provide all heat for pool from April to October. When pool reaches desired temperature, 700-gallon tank stores extra heat from panels to preheat household water and radiant space-heating system. Design: John Boyd.

Almost invisible against black roof of colonial-style house, 17 unglazed solar panels provide year-round heat for deep circular pool. Though most panels fit onto conveniently south-facing roof plane, some face east, with less desirable solar exposure. Large pump circulates water from pool up to high roof. Design: Fafco.

For super solar efficiency, south-facing solar panels heat black-bottomed pool. Pipes carry heated water from panels to pool equipment structure, then on to pool. Spa can be heated either with solar or conventional heater. Design: Sherwood Stockwell.

...solar-heated pools

Deck's pavement soaks up rays—a switch from the usual roof-top solar panels. Specially cast dark cement paving stones surround pool and collect sun's heat, as shown on page 31. Pipes in pavement circulate cool pool water through hot cement and return heated water to pool. Design: Don Brandeau.

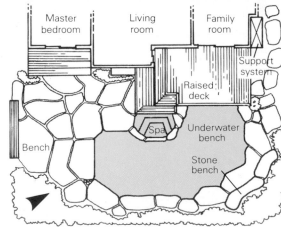

Versatility of fiberglass cover
makes investment worthwhile.
Cover collects sun's heat and maintains water at comfortable temperature for summer swimming. It also keeps debris out of water, is sturdy enough to walk on, and is sufficiently high to allow pool sweep to operate underneath. For swimming, owner can set cover at any of several positions to block wind or provide shade at poolside.
Design: Liftomatic.

ENCLOSED POOLS: ALL-YEAR SWIMMING

Pool came first. Then enclosure was built around part of existing garden. Indoor poolside landscaping is attractive result. Large fans keep air circulating in room; 8-foot doors all around enclosure can be opened to take advantage of breezes. Bridge across creek connects back patio of main house to pool house. Design: Tom Kessler.

It's a hop, skip, and a splash from house to enclosed pool and spa. Closed panels replace open screens on roof during winter for year-round exercise and relaxation. Brick coping and deck detail reflect brick construction of house. Design: John Withers, Master Pools by Geremia.

Dual-purpose glass and brick greenhouse shelters swimming pool and protects warmth-loving bougainvillea, banana, and hibiscus plants. during winter months. Timer automatically opens and closes vents in roof to control humidity. Long, shallow pool is perfect for lap swimming. Design: Lord & Burnham.

...enclosed pools

Like a giant balloon, air-inflated plastic enclosure covers pool for winter swimming, comes off in warm weather. Held up by air from a blower, spacious enclosure keeps inside warm and retains heat in water. Swimmers enter pool through a zippered door in plastic. Design: Air-Dome.

Family room connection to outdoor pool is long canal just wide enough for lap swimming. Floor is elevated above coping and protected from water by an edge of tile. Pool in shape of musical note shows owners' interest.

Enclosed pool doubles as a recreation room. Wood walls and ceiling, bold beams, and long skylight complement linear design of pool. Design: Marcel Breuer, Vera Neumann.

SPAS FOR A HOT-WATER SOAK

Radiating outward, wood decking creates space at poolside for sunning; deck also provides bridge to spa, built inside gunite pool. Underwater passages tunnel through base supporting spa. Design: Jones and Peterson.

Poolside geometry provides new angles for spa-pool-deck combination. Raised spa and deck conform to sloping contours of lot, and entire pool complex fits together like a modernistic puzzle. Design: Bob Maudsley, Peri-Bilt Pools.

Nestled in natural setting of giant ferns and lush foliage, poolside spa becomes a private escape for a hot soak. Flagstone slabs enclosing spa repeat flagstone pavement around pool. Design: Jack Buktenica.

Spa & Pool Combinations **59**

...hot-water spas

Canopy of vines supported on trellis secludes and screens poolside spa. Bathers in custom-made ceramic tile spa enjoy two venturi jets in each indented sitting area. Design: Don Boos.

Secluded spa tempts swimmers away from pool to bathe in forested splendor. Aggregate concrete decks overhang edges of pool and spa. Landscape design: Pacific Design Group. Pool and spa design: Sunsaver Pools.

Splash in the spa, then take a refreshing plunge into adjacent pool. Entire family enjoys proximity of hot spa and cooler pool. Multiple jets feed hot water to spa and keep it agitated. Overflow from spa goes directly into pool. Design: CSM Master Pools.

Spa & Pool Combinations **61**

CUSTOM TOUCHES

Poolside beach and rough-hewn boulders create seashore illusion. Beach is actually a gently sloping aggregate pavement reaching into water. Design: Galper Baldon & Associates.

For walking on water, swimmers cross steps supported on gunite bases built up from floor of pool. Step pads are made of same aggregate that surrounds pool. Design: Matsutani & Associates. Pool: Shelton's Custom Pools.

Aggregate, wood, and brick decks converge at poolside in carefully crafted linear design. Design: Philip S. Grimes.

Alaskan yellow cedar 2 by 4s separated by 1-inch cedar spacers are fashioned into an easy-to-hold handrail around edge of pool. Design: Don Brandeau.

...custom touches

Glistening waterfall washes over
concrete corner and adds sound
and movement to pool.
Design: Robert Babcock.

Rippling over rocks into pool, naturalistic waterfall circulates pool
water. Design: Zierden Waterfalls.
Pool: Master Pools by Geremia.

With a flip of a switch, automatic pool cover rolls out to cover pool or retracts out of sight under metal plate. Small wheels on both sides of cover keep it on track. Cover can be added to existing pools.

Hand-cranked insulating foam blanket unrolls to spread over pool, rolls back to uncover pool for swimming. Cover and frame assembly can be lifted and moved out of sight before visitors arrive.

DESIGNING FOR THE FUN OF IT

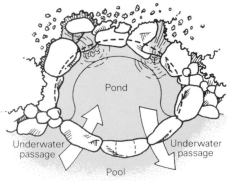

Secret hideaway—secluded pond with trickling waterfall—is youngsters' favorite. They reach it by swimming through underwater "cavern" from pool (at left) or by clambering over rocks (above). Design: John Withers, Master Pools by Geremia.

Like fish in an aquarium, swimmers are viewed by wine cellar visitors through underwater window. Made of 1-inch plate glass set in stainless steel frame, window is fastened to gunite pool shell with lagbolts. Steps by rail (left photo) lead down to cellar. Underwater windows give coaches a good view of diving and swimming techniques. Design: John Withers, Master Pools by Geremia.

Bright balloons of tile float on a sliding spillway and turn pool into a children's playground. Pool is also designed for safety: both spa and pool are shallow, and there's plenty of room to walk around pool. Design: Rod Garrett.

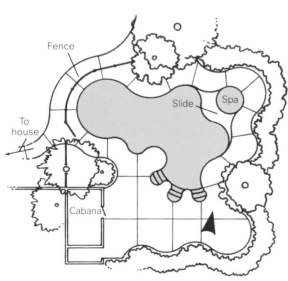

GREENING THE POOLSIDE

Like a mountain scene, lush greenery and isolated walkway (at left in photo) create woodland setting around oval vinyl-lined pool. Design: Hal Prince.

Preserving a grove of ash trees, pool conforms to existing landscape. Trees shed during autumn, so extra clean-up is required daily for about a month. Design: Dagmar Braun.

Maximum effect and minimum care—perfect combination is achieved here with daylily, asparagus fern, juniper, and star jasmine—plants that require little care and don't shed into water. Design: Tom Baak.

Riotously colorful and practical for poolside use, yellow gazanias and red aloe saponaria produce minimal litter for pool owner (or filter) to remove.

POOLSIDE PAVEMENTS

Accenting naturalistic design, flagstone deck of irregularly shaped and sized stone rims pool. Design: Tom Baak.

Hand-cut flagstone carefully laid on a bed of sand surrounds pool; rectangular concrete slab provides necessary support for diving board. Design: Buster Crabbe Pools of Newburgh.

Linear tile deck with integral coping complements rectangular pool and curved brickwork of wall and raised platform. Design: Bo Tegelvik.

Interlocking concrete blocks on a sand base provide both visual interest and a safe, nonskid surface at poolside. Design: Gene Kunit.

WOOD & WATER: DECK IDEAS FOR POOLS

Shaped to fit contours of hillside lot, dining deck under oak trees overlooks pool. On opposite side, redwood deck wraps around pool and extends out over hill. Design: Ronald Hermann, Carducci/Hermann Associates.

Reflecting elegance and simplicity of pool, raised redwood platform with built-in bench at rear cantilevers over water in both pool and spa. Square shape of platform repeats in other design elements. Design: Robert Royston, Royston, Hanamoto, Alley & Abey.

Artfully arranged base of boulders appears to be supporting redwood deck; actually, boulders conceal piers and footings under deck. Deck is constructed of alternating 2 by 2s and 2 by 6s laid in a parallel patten. Design: Lang & Wood.

POOLSIDE STRUCTURES

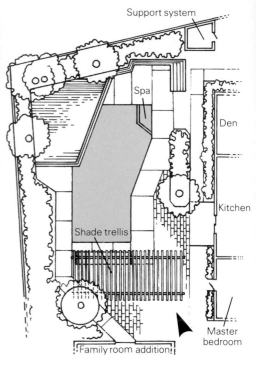

Support system

Spa

Den

Kitchen

Shade trellis

Master bedroom

Family room addition

Areas of sun and shade dapple poolside, but pool itself receives maximum sun all day. Lath patio roof casting shade on deck in foreground extends from family room. Underwater ledge below redwood deck protects swimmers from hitting their heads on overhang. Design: Don Brandeau.

Small but compact, cabana provides space for changing room, storage of garden equipment, shelves, wet bar, and covered seating. Pool design: Fred Fritsinger. Cabana: Fred Ackerman.

Raised, Oriental-inspired gazebo makes for a shady retreat from which to view pool in front and panorama behind. Design: Gene Kunit.

Arching bridge links patio to shady alcove on far side of pool and breaks long, freeform lap pool into two sections. Design: John Withers, Master Pools by Geremia.

POOLSIDE FENCES & SCREENS

Like a sentinel, wrought iron gate and fence with climbing star jasmine safely close off pool from grassy play area. Design: Duane Nelson, Nelson Aquatech Pools.

Decorative brick piers anchor wrought iron fence, separating pool from rest of yard but keeping it highly visible. Brick wall at left gives privacy to spa. Design: Mary Gordon.

Curved stockade-style fence reflects curves of pool and garden. Fence poles are nailed to both sides of frame constructed in short, straight sections. Design: Art Downing, Sherwood Stockwell.

Window-pane openings of trellis conceal door to master bedroom, yet allow pool to be viewed from inside. Design: Roy Rydell.

USING YOUR POOL FOR FITNESS & FUN

Ball sails over net held in place on poles embedded in concrete deck in this active game of water volleyball. Design: Galper Baldon & Associates.

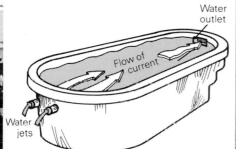

Swimming hard just to stay in place, swimmer works out against vigorous current produced by two jets. Each jet supplies 75 pounds per square inch of pressure at its nozzle; less powerful warm-water jets at opposite end of pool turn it into a spa. Design: Richard Murray. Pool: Aquaslide 'n Dive.

Floaters lend convenience for in-the-pool sports—basketball, volleyball, water polo. Lightweight and available commercially, nets go in the water for play, are easily removed when you want to swim.

BUILDING YOUR POOL

Having a pool built on your property is a major undertaking. By taking the time now to make very deliberate, tough decisions, you can, in the end, avoid delays, disappointment, and even financial loss.

You need to decide just how much you can afford to spend, to select a reputable builder you can work with, and to negotiate a contract that accurately describes what you want to build.

Of the three, choosing a pool builder is the most difficult and the most important. A reputable builder will assure you of a quality pool within your budget limitations. He or she will negotiate a contract with you that adequately describes your future pool and the work to be done. And finally, the pool builder will see that the work is done to your satisfaction.

YOUR BUDGET & YOUR POOL

Obviously, you'll want a quality pool, one that meets most if not all of your needs, at a price you can afford. Your costs will depend on the area you live in, the time of year, the type of pool, the quality of materials and workmanship, and the competitive market.

The way you arrange to have the pool built will also affect the costs. These are the options: you can let a landscape architect handle the whole project for you, you can contract directly with the builder, or you can do part or all of the work yourself.

A landscape architect not only can provide you with an integrated pool landscape design, but also can handle all the details of having the work done—negotiating contracts for you with the pool builder and any other contractor involved and overseeing their work. Though you'll pay more than if you dealt directly with the pool builder, the landscape architect gives you an original design and protects your interests.

Another possibility is to use the architect's design and work directly with the pool builder and other contractors yourself. But be prepared to spend considerable time and effort on the project.

Custom pool builders often can design not only the pool but also the surrounding landscaping. The builder can then do the entire job, or you can handle the landscaping yourself after the pool is completed. Either way will usually cost less than working with a landscape architect, but the design may lack some of the finer touches and the demand on your time will be greater.

Other pool builders may contract only for a pool selected from their available designs. This approach, at least initially, is the least costly, but you may not be as satisfied with the results. And you'll still be faced with the considerable effort and expense of landscaping the pool.

Building your own pool, usually vinyl-lined (see page 19), from a packaged pool kit is a possibility, particularly if you're competent at do-it-yourself projects and have some willing friends. You'll save money— but be prepared for a lot of hard work.

Some builders, if you convince them of your competence, may agree to your doing some of the pool building tasks and reduce the contract price accordingly. But you must be prepared to do the work when required or pay for delays on other parts of the project.

Stretching your dollars. Sometimes you can save money by contracting for a pool during a bargain season. Just when that is and how much you'll save depend on your location and the local competition. The bargain season in New England, the mid-Atlantic region, and the Midwest begins in July and

Rock outcroppings and abundant plantings disguise true nature of this spa and pool combination. Water at base of falls bubbles and foams in mock-wilderness splendor. Design: John Withers, Master Pools by Geremia. Waterfall: Zierden Waterfalls.

runs through early fall. Winter may bring some price reductions in the western and southern states, but the savings probably won't be nearly as great as in the colder areas.

CHOOSING A POOL PROFESSIONAL

Next to your home, and sending your children to college, your pool may well represent the biggest investment you'll make—reason enough to use great care in choosing the contractor who will build your pool.

It's best to get recommendations from pool-owning friends and neighbors who are satisfied with their pools and the people who built them. But even with the most glowing recommendations, it's important to check out all prospective builders. This will take time, as there are many ways to evaluate them. These are the principal ones:

• Visit the showrooms and offices of pool builders to get a feel for the business.

• If you're working with a landscape architect, ask for the names of several pool builders.

• Ask the companies you're considering for names and phone numbers of their customers. Five aren't enough, but 10 will be of some help, and 25 should give you a good sampling. If you can get 25 names, telephone 10 selected at random. Ask them how they feel about the builder, and if they're willing, look at their pools.

• Check for a company's membership in a trade association, such as the National Spa and Pool Institute (see page 16). Membership requires adherence to design and construction standards and a code of ethics. Many fine builders, though, don't belong.

• Call the Better Business Bureau. The quality of the information you receive varies; it can range from an evaluation of the builder's reputation to only an acknowledgment that the company is a member.

• Some local building departments will give you a list of pool permits issued for the year with the names and addresses of owners and builders. Call some of the owners and ask them about their experiences.

• Check the records in the county clerk's or recorder's office for any legal actions filed against companies you're considering. You'll probably have to search the records yourself, but you may find a friendly staff member to start you off. Several actions filed in a short period, or a continuous history of law suits, warrant further investigation. Your attorney may be able to give you some additional help in checking the contractors' legal history.

• Verify that the salesperson who calls on you actually works for the company he or she represents.

• Avoid companies whose sales staff pressures you to sign a contract. Any reputable company will give you adequate time to consider the proposed contract. Better not delay too long, though— you probably can't expect to make the same agreement 2 months after receiving the bid.

• Some lending institutions specialize in making pool loans through pool contractors. Usually, they're reluctant to make any meaningful comments about contractors to consumers. But you may be able to convince your personal banker to check for you.

• The company must be licensed by the state to build swimming pools. You may be able to check with the contractors' licensing board for specific information about the company.

• Find out whether the company uses its own men and equipment or hires subcontractors to do the work. You may get better service and fewer delays if the former is the case, since the company has complete control over the work and the schedule. But don't eliminate companies that subcontract much of their work for that reason alone; many small companies operate very efficiently this way.

Once you've considered all the information you've obtained, select three or four companies and ask them to submit bids on the pool you want. Unless you have definite opinions on the type of construction you want, choose these companies for their reputation, rather than for the type of pool they build.

Because of the many variables involved, try to have each builder you're considering bid on the exact same package. Then, if the companies are equally proficient, you'll be able to make a final choice on the basis of the bids they submit and the convenience of their construction schedules. But take your time, particularly if the bids vary widely.

If, on the other hand, the proposals don't include all the same elements, you'll have to take the differences into account when comparing bids. Study the proposals closely, and make sure you understand clearly what each builder is offering—and excluding. One basis for comparison is the price per square foot of swimming surface. Another is the quality and capacity of the support equipment. Sometimes a low price may cover just the basic pool, with extra costs for features that the bid for a higher-priced pool includes.

Neither automatically accept nor reject a bid that is unusually low. Instead, find out why. If the bidder forgot that you had mentioned boulders at the pool site, and you signed the contract knowing this, he or she could probably recover the added costs in court if you did not pay.

SIGNING THE CONTRACT

Without a signed contract between you and your builder, you'll both have nothing but trouble. A contract is an agreement between two parties covering the performance of certain work for a certain amount of money.

A good contract—whether it's the standard contract used by the builder or one prepared by your attorney—protects both your interests and the builder's. It must be tightly written, describing everything to be done and by whom, as well as everything not to be done. Don't sign it until you read and understand all of it.

"Musts" for the contract

A well-written, standard contract may cover both sides of a 14 by 18-inch sheet of paper in type considerably smaller than what you're reading. Any builder should be willing to give you a copy of the contract form in advance.

A contract should contain the following information:

Plans and specifications. These must be in sufficient detail so as to allow no question about what is to be built. A plan drawn to scale and attached to the contract should show the location of the pool on your property; the pool's shape, size, and dimensions; and the location of the support system, including filter and pump, solar panels (if any), heater, return lines, and main drain with pipe sizes, skimmers, and accessories.

Air-sprayed concrete (gunite) pools cannot be built to exact dimensions. The contract should contain a tolerance provision with a financial consideration for undersized and oversized dimensions. If a dimension comes out smaller than what you contracted for, you get a rebate. If larger, you pay an additional fee. If your tolerance is 5 percent over or under, the dimension on a 40-foot-long pool can vary from 38 to 42 feet.

Performance. The contract should specify all the work to be done, materials to be used, equipment to be installed (including manufacturer and model number), and any optional features to be considered. The date work will start and end should be stated (unless local weather conditions do not allow it), as well as the time when the owner becomes responsible for maintenance. It should also lay down conditions for suspension, arbitration, and termination (under federal law,

you are allowed 3 business days after signing the contract to change your mind).

Excavation and grading. The contract should state the costs of gaining access to the site, relocating utilities, and excavation of unknown underground hazards whether man-made or natural. It should also assign responsibility for final grading and for the removal of building debris and surplus earth and rock.

Costs and payment. Outlined in the contract should be the cost of the specified work and any options, the payment schedule (a series of payments based on work completed), and the question of ownership in the case of bankruptcy.

Consider the payment schedule carefully. On the one hand, to ensure that you won't have paid in full for an uncompleted pool, you may want to make partial payments as different stages of the work are completed. The builder, on the other hand, would prefer to be paid before the work is completed, in order to be paid in full by the time the job is finished. At least one state, California, has passed a law preventing the pool owner from being forced to pay for work not completed.

Legal conditions. Legal provisions in the contract should include the validity period for the agreed-upon price, responsibility for permits and zoning compliance, and provisions for mechanic's lien releases as the labor and materials used are paid for (these come from the contractor and any subcontractors and material suppliers involved). Why are these releases necessary? Because even though you've paid the contractor, if he or she has not paid those who have done work or supplied material on your property, under mechanic's lien laws you can be liable for the amount they are owed. In addition to requiring lien releases every time you make a payment, you can request that the pool builder post a bond assuring payment to subcontractors.

Liability for damages and personal injury and guarantee provisions for the contractor's work and any equipment installed should also be written into the contract. Under federal law, you must be advised that equipment warranties are available, and you must be given the opportunity to examine them.

GUIDE TO POOL CONSTRUCTION

Think of pool construction as being divided into two main phases—the building of the basic shell that holds the water and the application of the finish and trim.

Building the shell is by far the most crucial element; it will determine both the usefulness and the longevity of your pool. The engineering, design, and skilled work required leave no room for short cuts or economizing that could result in maintenance problems or actual failure of the pool.

On the other hand, choosing and applying the finish does permit some variation. In plaster or paint, tile, coping, and decking, you can select materials for economy, color, and personal taste. But be sure never to compromise on the construction methods. Finish and trim should be applied with the same care used to build the basic shell. In addition to being decorative, some of these finishing touches contribute to the structural integrity of the pool.

This section is not a build-it-yourself construction manual. Rather, it will guide you through the construction process so you can better understand what's going on while the pool builders are at work. You may find variations in these procedures because of climatic conditions, special structural requirements, and differences among contractors.

Site preparation and excavation

Excavating for an in-ground pool or grading a level area for an on-ground pool is the first step in the actual building of your pool. Normally, the excavated material is trucked away, but if you want to use some for landscaping, arrange with the builder beforehand. You may even save some money.

Layout.   Working from the plan that's in the contract, the builder will establish the finished grade level, taking into account the thickness of the deck and slopes for drainage.

The outline of the pool is then marked with stakes. A digging line which takes into account the thickness of the walls and any additional space required is indicated on the ground with wood strips staked into place or with flour, lime, or some other white powder.

The rough excavation.   After the digging line has been marked, the rough excavation begins. Excavators normally use a back hoe or a front-end loader with this operation; the equipment needs an 8 to 10-foot-wide access. Excavators

Back hoe (shown here) or front-end loader usually digs pool excavation.

like to come in at the shallow end of the pool for ease of operation, but if the only reasonable path is through the deep end, this causes no more trouble than extra stacking of sand bags to fill in the hole in the pool wall that's needed to move the back hoe in and out of the deepening excavation.

Finishing.   The back hoe or loader can cut only to within 6 inches of the pool perimeter; the final shaping and finishing must be done by hand. The finishing should be done while the back hoe is making the rough cut; this way, all the dirt that is cut away in finishing can be moved out of the pool immediately.

There are two general types of excavations: those which follow the exact lines of the pool and must be carefully hand-trimmed (gunite and some fiberglass pools), and those which can be overexcavated on the sides—but not the bottom —and then backfilled after the pool has been installed (poured concrete, masonry block, and vinyl-lined pools).

With the latter type, the first finishing job is to establish the correct depths and slope of the pool. The excavation for a vinyl-lined pool must fit the liner exactly.

For gunite and fiberglass pools, the finishing process is especially important. The shell follows the contours of the excavation exactly, and errors in the finishing will show up as errors in the finished pool.

With fiberglass, the fitting of the pool into the excavation is the most critical point of the installation. Care must be taken not to overexcavate; if this does happen, a concrete mix rather than loose dirt will probably be required for backfill material.

For steel-reinforced concrete pools, walls are usually vertical for 3 feet and then begin to taper into 5-foot-radius corners. This gives straight sides to the shallowest part of the pool and a bowl effect to the deep end.

Problem soils.   In excavating, there are only three types of problem soil—wet, rock, and sand. All three are solvable but will add to your costs.

Wet soil is a problem because the loader can't move about freely, the walls sag, and the finishing can't be done. The usual solution is to pump the water out of the pool while the loader moves in and out, the finishing work is completed, and the main drain set; even then,

it may be necessary to continue pumping water out of the main drain until the concrete is in.

If the wet soil prevents the loader from entering the pool at all, it may be a good reason for not building the pool, unless adequate drainage is arranged to keep water pressure away from the bottom of the pool.

Rock requires expensive drilling and blasting; a loader must be kept on the job to move the rock as it's chipped away. But rock can be an advantage, since it provides a solid foundation for the pool.

With sand, the excavator may have trouble with the walls caving in as the excavation deepens. There is usually a stopping point for cave-ins, but if the trouble persists, a thin coat of gunite can be sprayed on the walls to shore them up until the pool shell is built.

Special soil conditions

If your pool site has some special soil condition—underground water pressure from a high water table, expansive soil, fill, or rock—your pool contractor will need to take special measures to deal with it.

Underground water pressure. The problem of underground water pressure exists with all pools with rigid floors. The pool is basically a giant saucer and can be pushed upward if enough water pressure is allowed to collect beneath the pool. This is particularly dangerous when the pool is empty, since there's no weight to counteract the pressure.

To avoid this problem, most pool builders install hydrostatic valves at the main drain of concrete, fiberglass, and hybrid fiberglass pools. These valves open either automatically or manually to relieve the pressure by allowing ground water to enter the pool.

Manual valves (with a handle similar to a water faucet handle) remain closed while the pool is full and there is little danger of buoyancy. But when the pool is either partially or completely drained, a long forked pole is used to open the valve, releasing the hydrostatic pressure. When the pool is refilled, the valve is closed.

Hydrostatic valves are equipped with a float that's raised by water pressure from below. This prevents water from leaking out of the pool. Only when the pressure beneath becomes great enough to lift the float will the valve open.

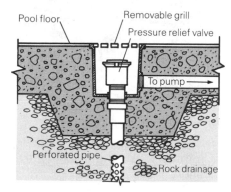

If your pool doesn't have a hydrostatic valve, the pool should never be drained without first contacting the contractor or an engineer. They will advise when the water table is low enough to avoid a dangerous pressure build-up.

Where valves are not used (and in all cases where there is likely to be a very heavy build-up of underground water), a subgrade drainage system should be installed. The pool can be ringed with a line of drain tile, placed on a definite grade for good drainage. The floor of concrete and fiberglass pools should rest on a bed of crushed rock, if surrounding soils are normally slow-draining.

Expansive soil. Generally, expansive soil resists water, but when it finally does absorb moisture, the earth expands a lot. As a result, heavy pressure builds up against the pool walls and may crack them.

Pool builders generally have two sets of steel plans, one for normal soil and one for expansive soil. The latter calls for more reinforcing steel, thicker walls, or both. But since the walls are rigid, there is still a danger of cracking if the soil expansion is uneven or greater than anticipated.

An expandable water stop can be installed to prevent water from

seeping into the soil at the joint between the coping-bond beam section and the deck. Made of rubber or plastic, the stop can take several forms. The usual type, called a compressible expansion joint, is poured as a liquid into a gap prepared for it between the deck and coping when the deck is laid. When the joint dries, it forms a tight, flexible seal. If decks are laid out in sections, the joints must also be sealed for several feet around the pool.

Your contractor can take additional preventive measures, often used together to insure protection.

• A 6-inch lip can be poured on the back edge of the surrounding walkway to provide extra support for the bond beam.

• The top 3 feet of clay around the pool can be replaced with clean, compacted fill; this lessens the pressure by removing the cause. In some cases, as with fiberglass, the backfill is reinforced cement grout to give the shell even more rigid support.

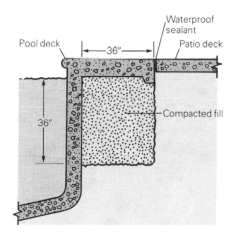

• A trench, 4 feet deep and 12 inches wide, can be dug around the pool, 5 to 10 feet from the walls. This is filled with loose material that can absorb the soil expansion; the top of the trench can be covered with decking later.

Fill. A few feet of fill on the top layer of an excavation, or perhaps a thin layer deeper in the hole, is not a problem. But if the entire excavation is loose fill, the pool will not have a footing in solid earth and will

float in the fill. When the fill, compressed by the pool's weight, settles, the pool settles with it. If the settling is uniform, the pool pulls away from the bond beam and cracks; if it's uneven, the pool will crack crosswise at approximately the 5-foot depth mark.

To give the pool a solid footing in deep fill, the contractor can use caisson construction, building the pool shell on piers or pilings sunk into solid ground. The piers are made of concrete and reinforcing steel rods. The rods extend into the pool shell and are fastened to the reinforcing steel in the shell. Even though the fill may compact and leave a space under the shell, the integrated construction of the piers and the pool shell prevents any damage or movement.

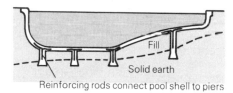

Reinforcing rods connect pool shell to piers

Rock. Normal granitelike rock requires expensive excavation but makes a fine bed for a swimming pool. Holes are drilled in the rock for explosive charges. After the explosion, the shattered rock is removed from the excavation.

Slate, shale, and gravel, on the other hand, tend to move and slide when wet and can impose great forces on the pool. To eliminate these forces, you'll need extra retaining walls and perhaps a backfilling of solid earth.

How a contractor builds a pool

It's helpful to know what to expect—and what to look for—after the digging stops and the builder begins work on your pool. Starting on the next page, you'll find the major steps in the construction of gunite, vinyl-lined, and fiberglass pools. Be aware that the actual sequence of the steps can differ between contractors.

(Continued on next page)

For a **gunite pool,** these construction steps will follow the excavation.

• Plumbing pipes that will be inaccessible once the concrete is poured are installed.

• A gravel bed is laid in the bottom of the excavation.

• Reinforcing rods and forms for the bond beam are installed.

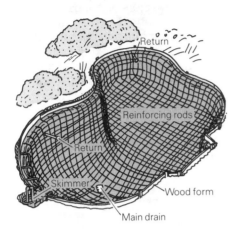

• The rough plumbing—main drain, skimmers, in-wall cleaner (if used), and stubs for the returns—is set down.

• Niches and electrical conduit for underwater lights are put in place.

• Concrete is sprayed on walls and floor, and on steps, seats, and connected spa (if any).

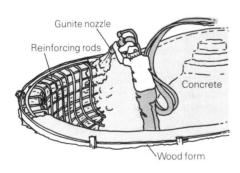

• Concrete is cleaned out of light niches, main drain, returns, and other openings.

• Concrete is troweled to a smooth finish if surface is to be painted.

• Coping is built around rim of pool. The coping may be precast,

brick, flagstone, or tile, as shown below, or be formed by the edge of a concrete deck.

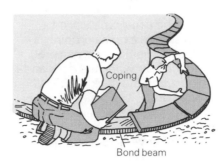

• Tile is applied to the water line and, if specified, to the steps, spa, coping, ledges, sides, and bottom of the pool.

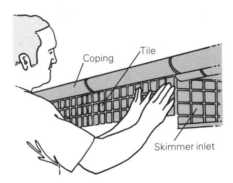

• After concrete is cured, plaster is applied and troweled to a smooth finish, or concrete is painted.

• After plaster is cured or paint is dry, pool is filled with water, support equipment is hooked up and turned on, and water is treated with chemicals.

A **vinyl-lined pool** is built in the manner described below.

• Footing for sidewall panels is leveled.

• Sidewalls are erected, bolted together, and anchored in place with concrete.

• Rough plumbing for main drain, skimmers, returns, and floor-type cleaners (if used) is installed.

• Sand or other suitable material is spread in bottom and leveled or contoured as required.

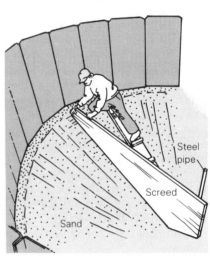

• Liner is spread over sidewalls, lowered into position, and fastened to top of sidewalls.

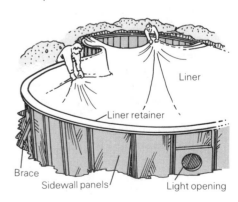

- Coping is attached.
- While pool is being filled, liner is smoothed out, openings cut, and main drain, skimmers, returns, and lights are installed.
- Plumbing and electrical work is completed and support system hooked up.

The site for a *fiberglass pool* is excavated before the shell makes its dramatic entrance. The work proceeds as follows:
- Rough plumbing under pool is installed.
- Sand is spread in bottom of excavation and contoured to fit pool shell.
- Shell is lifted off truck and lowered into excavation.

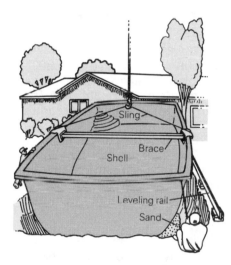

- Shell is leveled and adjusted to proper grade; temporary braces supported on wood rails on each side of pool hold shell in position.

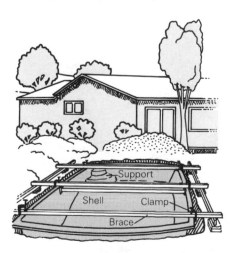

- Rough plumbing is connected to main drain, floor-type cleaners (if used), skimmers, and returns.
- Excavation is backfilled with sand, and at the same time, pool is filled with water.
- Plumbing and electrical work is completed and support system is hooked up.
- Backfilling is finished, sand is compacted, and deck is graded.
- Forms for deck are prepared.
- Concrete deck is poured and finished.

Pool finishes and trims

Depending on the type of pool you're building, you can choose the materials and colors for pool finishes and trims—paint or plaster, tile, and coping.

Interior finishes. Vinyl-lined and fiberglass pools need no interior finish. All others must be plastered or painted (tile is another type of finish, but is seldom used for residential pools because of the high cost of materials and labor). Paint can be applied by the homeowner; plastering is a professional job. Consult a reliable paint manufacturer before deciding whether to paint your pool yourself. Paint applied to a surface that will be underwater must be handled very carefully.

In most parts of the United States, it's less expensive to paint than to plaster a pool, but in mild climates a carefully maintained plaster finish may last indefinitely; a painted pool requires additional coats every few years.

Plaster is the most common finish used on concrete pools; it gives a smooth waterproof skin to the pool, and provides a nonskid walking surface on the bottom of the pool.

Though most concrete pools are finished in white plaster, a mixture of white cement and white marble dust, other colors are increasing in popularity.

To avoid gouging the plaster when the pool is filled, most builders recommend using a garden hose with the nozzle placed on the main drain. When the water is

about 3 feet deep, several hoses can be used, providing the incoming flow falls on water rather than plaster.

Coping. Coping gives the pool a good finish—it covers the round concrete edges of the bond beam, conceals the steel projecting from pool walls into the deck, integrates the interior finish and tile of the pool, and emphasizes the lines of the pool.

Coping also serves as a nonskid surface for walking and diving, a hand hold for swimmers, and a smooth sitting bench or shove-off point into the water. When coping is correctly installed, water splashed out of the pool or carried out by dripping swimmers should flow away from the pool and into drainage channels in the deck.

Precast coping stones in straight lengths, corners, and curved sections are the most economical type of coping. The stones are usually made from colored concrete with a porous finish.

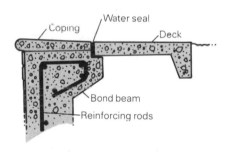

Instead of using coping stones, you can simply extend a concrete or wood deck to the edge of the pool and even slightly over the edge.

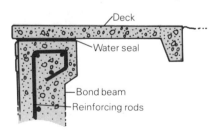

Or you can use flagstone, brick, or other masonry materials. Be sure to trim and buff the edges of any naturally rough stone to a smooth finish. Make the overhanging portion thin enough for a convenient hand hold.

Diving boards, slides, ladders, and grab rails make using your pool more enjoyable and convenient. Other accessories—support system controls, chemical dispensers and automatic cleaners—reduce the time you spend maintaining your pool. Though some can be added to an existing pool, most accessories need to be incorporated into your initial pool design.

Diving boards

One of the most popular pool accessories, a diving board must be securely anchored to the deck. In addition, the pool must be sufficiently long, deep, and wide for the length of the planned board and its height above the water. The National Spa and Pool Institute has developed a residential pool standard (summarized in the table below) for the use of diving boards in home pools (see page 16). It's important to follow these standards to avoid injury to divers.

DIVING SAFETY GUIDE

NSPI pool type	Minimum depth at deepest point	Minimum width at deepest point	Minimum pool length	Maximum diving board length	Maximum jump board length	Maximum board height above water
II	7½ ft.	15 ft.	28 ft.	8 ft.	6 ft.	20 in.
III	8 ft.	15 ft.	30 ft.	10 ft.	8 ft.	26 in.
IV	8½ ft.	18 ft.	33 ft.	12 ft.	8 ft.	30 in.
V	9 ft.	18 ft.	36 ft.	12 ft.	8 ft.	40 in.

If your pool is smaller than type II , it's not safe to have a board.

Fiberglass is the most common material for diving boards, though you can use wood or aluminum as well. The fiberglass boards have either a laminated wood core or wood stringers embedded in the fiberglass. Be sure the top of the board has a nonslip coating or a nonslip material cemented to it.

The longer the diving board, the more space you'll need for it at poolside. If space is limited, consider a jump stand anchored to the deck. The jump stand board is short, and the springing action is achieved by the use of heavy springs between the board and deck. Even a jump stand board should conform to the NSPI standards for pool depth, width, and length.

Pool slides

Pool slides are great fun—good enough reason for their increasing popularity among the young set. A pool slide, like a diving board, must be securely anchored to the deck. You'll also want to adhere to the NSPI standard for placement and pool size and depth.

Slides are made of fiberglass with a gelcoat finish and are supported on a metal frame. The higher the slide, the longer it must be. A straight slide 7 feet high will be about 13 feet long and will require a deck width of over 15 feet. If your deck space is limited, you can use a slide that curves to the left or right. A curved slide 7 feet high needs a deck width of only 3½ feet. The higher the slide, the deeper the water must be, and the more open space you'll need in front of it.

Ladders & grab rails

Though your pool probably has steps at the shallow end, you'll want a convenient way, or even two, to get out of the pool at the deep end. You can install a stainless steel ladder (see below). If you have a concrete pool, build steps into the side of the pool and flank them with a pair of grab rails. A grab rail near the steps at the shallow end is also convenient.

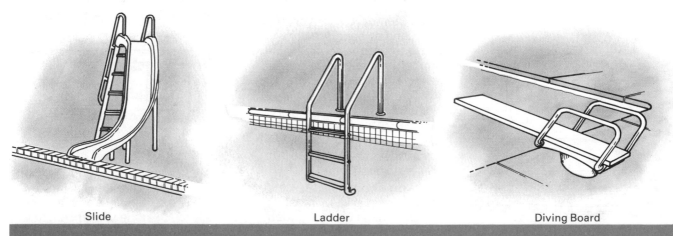

Slide   Ladder   Diving Board

Automatic controls

Automatic controls added to your pool system can take over such chores as turning the support system on and off, backwashing the filter, and maintaining the chlorine level.

Automatic timer.   Basically a 24-hour electric clock with adjustable contacts, a timer turns equipment on and off at preset times. You can use a timer to turn on the heater, the pump for the filtration system, and the pump for an automatic pool cleaner (see below). You can also control the heater with a thermostat to maintain the pool water at the desired temperature. Remember that whenever the heater is on, the pump must also be running; after the heater shuts off, keep the pump running long enough to clear all hot water from the pipes.

Backwashing the filter.   You can eliminate the chore of backwashing your sand filter by installing an electronic device that monitors the increasing pressure in the system due to dirt; when the pressure is high enough to warrant backwashing, the device activates the necessary valves to do the job.

Dispensing chemicals.   Dispensers for chemicals and disinfectants range from a simple floating type containing pellets or sticks to one that manufactures chlorine and dispenses it automatically. Ask your pool builder, pool service company, or pool supply store for information and advice. Even with an automatic dispenser, you'll need to test your pool water regularly and add supplemental chemicals as needed.

Pool cleaners

Automatic pool cleaners work either by vacuuming the dirt off the pool bottom or by agitating the dirt so it's carried out through the main drain. The cleaner's pump may be separate from the filtration system or connect directly into the filtration system.

Vacuum system.   Seemingly with a mind of its own, a vacuum cleaner wanders in a random pattern across the bottom of the pool and sucks up dirt. The dirt-laden water is then carried through a flexible hose into the pool filtration system.

Agitators.   One type of agitating cleaner floats on the surface of the pool and propels itself around. Trailing from it are two or more hoses that swirl around under the force of water being pumped out of their ends. Another kind of agitating cleaner also uses hoses with water jets, but the hoses are built into the sides of the pool and retract when not in use. A third type of cleaner returns the water from the filtration system through special jets built into the bottom of the pool; the jets direct the water over the bottom of the pool and move dirt towards the main drain.

AUTOMATIC POOL CLEANERS

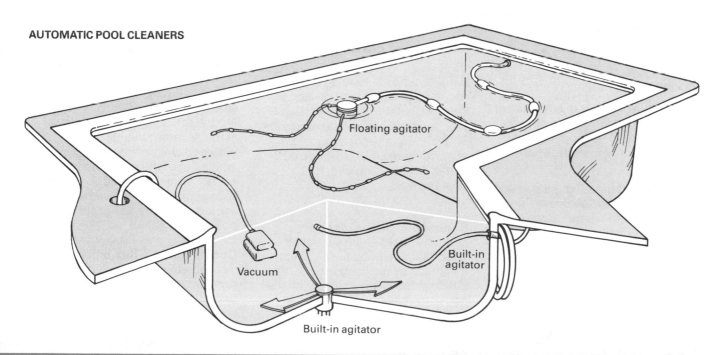

Floating agitator

Vacuum

Built-in agitator

Built-in agitator

LANDSCAPING YOUR POOL

Whether you're landscaping a pool from scratch, remodeling what's already in place, or just contemplating the task for the future, designing a successful pool landscape demands the same careful planning that went into building your pool.

There's more to a pool setting than just the pool, a lawn, and a few scattered plants. Instead, good pool landscaping involves arranging and integrating many diverse elements—plantings, fences, walls, pavements, structures, and lighting, as well as the pool and its decking.

And don't forget to put yourself into the picture. Your pool environment should reflect your personal tastes and accommodate your needs.

You'll find gardening ideas and techniques in the following *Sunset* books: *Western Garden Book, Landscaping & Garden Remodeling, Landscaping Illustrated,* and *Basic Gardening.*

For outdoor building information, consult these *Sunset* books: *Decks; Patios & Decks; Fences & Gates; Walks, Walls & Patio Floors; Spas, Hot Tubs & Home Saunas; Basic Masonry Illustrated;* and *Garden & Patio Building Book.*

BASIC LANDSCAPE PRINCIPLES

Landscape architects and designers rely on several fundamental principles, when they're designing a landscaping plan. You, too, can master these principles and then use them to develop your own effective pool landscape.

Landscaping goals

A successful landscape scheme has as its goals beauty, privacy, comfort, safety, convenience and flexibility, and ease of maintenance. Though you may not be able to achieve them all, you'll come out ahead if you design with these goals in mind.

Beautify.   You may consider a beautiful pool setting almost as important as a good swim. Create this mood by blending the pool and other landscape elements with the house to achieve an esthetic balance throughout the whole area.

Privacy.   If privacy is your primary concern, include trees, fences, walls, screens, or hedges in your plan to block the view of the pool area from the street or a neighbor's windows.

Comfort.   For swimming, sunning, or entertaining by the pool, you'll be more comfortable in a setting that's been adjusted for particular climatic conditions. You'll need room for lounging around the pool, as well as the right combination of design elements to modify sun or wind.

Safety.   Planning a safe pool area—not only for your own family but for your neighbors as well—needs to have high priority. Self-closing gates and safety fencing around the pool (required by law in many communities) or yard will keep children, pets, and even adults out of the pool when you are not around. Passageways near your pool need to be well defined, lighted at night, and not slippery or obstructed.

Convenience & flexibility.   Try to incorporate into your plan areas for pool-related activities like cooking, eating, entertaining, showering, and changing. The more convenient to the pool these facilities are, the more you'll enjoy your pool without worrying about traffic in and out of your house.

Give landscape elements multiple jobs: design built-in benches that also store pool furniture, sports gear, or garden equipment; install adjustable screens that provide shade and block the wind and undesirable views; build a covered firepit that doubles as a sunning deck or low table. Easy access to your pool from more than one of your main living areas also gives flexibility.

Ease of maintenance. With ever-rising maintenance costs, you'll want to choose materials very carefully. Consider using wood that doesn't need constant repainting or staining, masonry surfaces that need no painting, rustproof furniture, and trees and shrubs that drop a minimum of leaves and flowers.

Ground rules for landscaping

As you plan your pool setting it may be helpful to think in terms of four basic landscape goals: unity, balance, variety, and proportion.

Unity in a pool setting is achieved when everything looks as though it belongs together. No landscape element stands out; each blends with the other parts, as well as with the house and the lot.

To achieve unity, avoid designing too many distinctive units that will have to be tied together. The more units you divide your landscape into, the harder it will be to create unity.

Balance—not to be confused with symmetry—does a lot to make a pool setting pleasing. Most likely, your pool will be the focal point of your landscape design. Achieve balance by combining design elements that produce the same visual weight on either side of this center of interest. A large tree or structure on one side of the pool, for example, can be balanced with a grouping of smaller trees on the other.

But don't try to make these relationships too equal. Remember that mass isn't the only expression of visual weight; it can be ex-

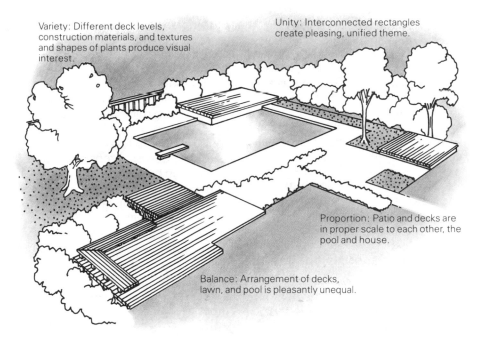

Variety: Different deck levels, construction materials, and textures and shapes of plants produce visual interest.

Unity: Interconnected rectangles create pleasing, unified theme.

Proportion: Patio and decks are in proper scale to each other, the pool and house.

Balance: Arrangement of decks, lawn, and pool is pleasantly unequal.

pressed with color, form, or interest, as well.

Variety breaks up what could be monotonous unity. Differing but complementary grade levels, construction materials, textures, colors, and shapes arouse visual interest both horizontally and vertically.

Vary an expanse of pavement with two different paving materials, such as wood and exposed aggregate concrete. Plant shrubs in groupings of various heights and colors.

Proportion demands that the various forms, materials, and open spaces of your landscape be in scale with one another. Nothing looks more out of place than a small pool in a yard as flat and expansive as a football field, or an oversized patio that looks more like a parking lot than an entertainment area.

Landscape elements need to be in scale not only with one another, but also with your house, lot, and pool.

If your lot is extremely large, try breaking the space up into several distinct areas. Screens, plantings, patios, or walks become borders or barriers that can divide your yard into intimate areas.

To maintain proportion in a small lot, keep the design simple

and uncluttered. Tall vertical screens used to enclose a small area will actually make it seem larger, as will solid paving. Use plants with restraint—overplanting will just add clutter.

When selecting plantings, keep their ultimate sizes and shapes in mind. Though a plant when young may suit the proportion of your lot, it may grow far too tall for it within a few years.

Basic design techniques

Landscape architects and designers use some basic design techniques that you can borrow in thinking about your own design. These can make the difference between a visually pleasing landscape or an awkward, jarring one.

• If the relationship between elements in your landscape is either too equal or extremely unequal, the result can be visually disturbing.

• When organizing space, remember that most people find a sense of order in well-known, simple shapes, such as squares, rectangles, triangles, and circles.

• Arrange plantings and structures to satisfy the need for privacy, but don't carry the design so far that it will produce a cooped-up feeling.

• You can create pleasing variations in the landscape design and yet maintain unity by carrying a recognizable shape through a main theme. A theme with variations—in pavement, overhead, fence, lawn, and raised flower bed—creates a unified landscape.

• In grouping shapes or masses, make them seem unified by joining or interlocking the units, rather than separating them.

• The safe way to create a visually unified landscape is to compose a rhythmic pattern of the landscape elements.

Challenging landscaping sites

Like everything else in nature, lots are not all perfect. One of the secrets of landscaping—whether you're starting from scratch or restoring a well-worn yard—is knowing how to turn liabilities into assets. You will find more information beginning on page 12.

Small sites. Function needs to be your foremost consideration in landscaping a small area. Besides swimming, will it be used for entertaining, sunning, or play; it can also just be admired for its esthetic qualities.

Even in a small site, careful planning can create the illusion of space. Brick paving, with its small-scale, repetitive pattern, gives an expansive feeling. To save space, display plants in small beds, containers, or hanging baskets.

Built-in storage and seating are practically a must where space is limited. Choose furnishings that don't overpower their surroundings, and avoid clutter at all costs.

Sloping sites. Whether your lot is gently sloping, extremely steep, or somewhere in between, you will have to meet special design requirements.

A shallow slope can be converted with a minimum of grading into two or more level areas. Steps and a raised planting bed serve as retaining walls. Steps, ramps, or both can provide the transition from one level to another. Grass or ground cover can be used on slightly sloping sites to prevent erosion in large unpaved areas.

A medium slope is improved when it's graded to form a series of gradual levels, each marked by a retaining wall and planted with ground cover.

A steep slope is conquerable, in many cases, by a deck built beside the pool. Steep, difficult slopes often require the attention of professional landscape architects.

Besides their purely functional use in providing a connection between different levels, steps and ramps play a major role in both grading the site and integrating buildings into the landscape. They also separate areas, direct foot traffic, display plantings, and on occasion, even provide extra seating.

Odd-shaped sites. The four basic types of odd-shaped lots are square, wedge-shaped, wide and shallow, and long and narrow. Turn to page 13 for additional ways to handle these odd-shaped lots; you'll also find complete illustrations of the lots of which only portions are shown at right.

A square lot's symmetry is softened by an elliptical pool and a separate landscaped area behind the house.

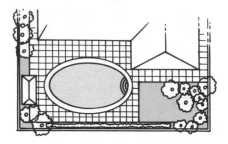

A wide and shallow lot appears deeper when the area behind the house is broken up into a series of outdoor living areas: a long, narrow pool (shown below), a large patio for entertaining, and a circular sitting area shaded by trees.

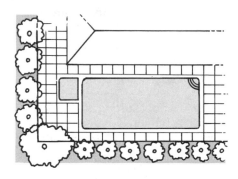

A wedge-shaped lot's primary drawbacks are its sharply angled corners and unequally divided spaces. Plants can camouflage the sharp corners. Locating the swimming pool in the large open area contributes to the secluded nature of the adjoining smaller garden (see next page).

SLOPING SITES

Steep slope   Medium slope   Shallow slope

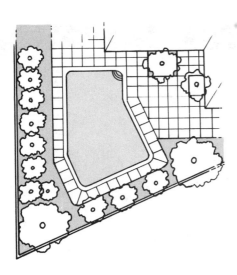

A deep, narrow lot can be divided into two distinct areas— a large patio and a very private, naturalistic pool site beyond. A modest grade adds visual interest.

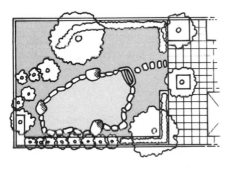

LANDSCAPING DESIGN ELEMENTS

The scope of landscaping elements available to you is as broad as your imagination. Here we've presented those most crucial to the success of your pool landscape—plantings, fences, masonry walls, vertical and horizontal screens, decks and pavement, poolside structures, and finishing touches such as lights.

You'll discover that these can be used in many different ways— some will work for you, others won't. Let your needs, your budget, and your personal taste determine your final choices. And be sure not to ignore code requirements and professional advice.

How you combine the ele-ments is just as important as the ones you choose. They should not only complement each other, but also harmonize with the pool, the lot, and the house itself.

Planting around the pool

Plants around the pool add color, texture, shape, and interest to the pool landscape, besides creating a beautiful, natural setting for the pool.

Moreover, plants provide privacy and security. Trees, dense hedges, or vines, when grown over a support, hide unwanted views. Tough plant borders or barriers can prevent pets and people from walking across lawns or plant beds. Prickly or thorny plantings can discourage trespassers from climbing the walls or fences, but you won't want them near the pool or lounging areas.

Plants are thermal tools that insulate the pool area: grass and ground covers cool; trees, plant screens, and hedges cool and shade; deciduous trees provide summer sun and wind protection and allow winter sunlight to filter through their branches; evergreen trees provide year-round shade and wind protection.

Plants are even good cover-ups. Use them to soften architectural lines, hide construction flaws, camouflage pool equipment, and fill in odd angles on your lot.

Plants must be suited to their climate zone. For examples of poolside plants that will thrive in your climate, see pages 94–95.

Planting considerations. If

you've ever had to pluck plant debris out of a pool, you'll understand the reluctance of many pool owners to plant anything next to the pool. But plants play a vital role in the pool environment. Choosing plant materials and the location of planting beds very carefully will produce the attractive pool landscape you want and ensure minimum maintenance.

Successful plantings require adequate drainage. Water from the pool, from rain, and from the hose you use to clean off paved areas must go somewhere, and since most pool decking is graded away from the pool itself, that water will run off into your plantings.

Lawns, ground covers, and other plants can absorb quantities of water, but the first foot or two of space adjacent to paved areas often receives more than its share. To protect this area from becoming saturated and boggy, channel the water before it reaches the plant materials by using gutters.

Selection of plants. Installing a pool will affect the climate in your yard—the expanse of water, especially if the pool is heated, produces high humidity. Plants susceptible to mildew are likely to be affected. In making new selections, choose plants that will withstand moisture.

If your pool site is surrounded by pines or other conifers, oaks, or eucalyptus, all of which shed the year around, consider a screened enclosure for the entire pool and deck area. Otherwise you'll have to accept the debris problem. Sometimes pool owners who want the benefits of trees plant deciduous kinds, preferring a big leaf drop once a year to the small but continuous leaf drop of many evergreens.

Keep any new tree plantings away from the pool, if possible. Also, be sure you know how far their root systems are likely to spread, so you won't get roots in your water pipes.

Don't plant any fruit-bearing shrubs or trees near the pool deck. The dropping fruit becomes slippery and can even stain the deck; it also attracts bees, yellow jackets, and other insects.

Around the pool, choose plants that drop a minimum of leaves, seeds, resin, and other debris; avoid any that attract stinging insects or birds. And if you're fond of shrubs with thorns or barbs, plant them well away from the area.

Unhappily, some of the worst litterers are also among the best-looking plants around a pool— bamboo and pampas grass, for

(Continued on page 96)

POOLSIDE PLANTS

The plants listed below are some that are happy growing near swimming pools. The map at right indicates climate zones keyed to the plant list below. If you want a more detailed map of your growing area, you can obtain the Plant Zone Hardiness Map from the United States Department of Agriculture. This map divides the United States and Canada into 10 temperature zones and shows the boundaries of all U.S. counties in relation to those zones.

To determine the precise growing requirements of the plants for your area, consult your local nursery or a regional growing guide, such as *Sunset's Western Garden Book*.

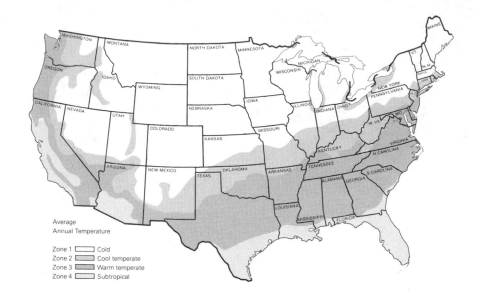

Average
Annual Temperature

Zone 1 ▭ Cold
Zone 2 ▨ Cool temperate
Zone 3 ▨ Warm temperate
Zone 4 ▭ Subtropical

GROUND COVERS

Name of Plant	Evergreen or Deciduous	Climate Zones	Remarks
AGAPANTHUS 'Peter Pan'	E	4	Good for containers, borders.
AJUGA reptans		1–4	Perennial; fast spreading; makes thick carpet.
CERASTIUM tomentosum		1–4	Perennial; cascades in rock gardens, patterns, fillers, borders.
COTONEASTER adpressus	D	1–4	Slow growing; follows contours of ground, rocks.
DIANTHUS deltoides		1–4	Perennial; use for borders, rock gardens.
HELIANTHEMUM nummularium	E	1–4	Rambles in rock gardens, on slopes.
HYPERICUM calycinum	E	2–4	Controls hillside erosion.
IBERIS sempervirens	E	1–4	Good for borders, rock gardens, containers.
JUNIPERUS chinensis sargentii	E	1–4	Slow growing; use for borders, rock gardens; controls erosion.
MENTHA requienii		2–4	Perennial; fast-spreading herb with mossy effect; keep in bounds.
PACHYSANDRA terminalis	E	1–4	Transition between walks, lawns, shrubs.
SAGINA subulata		1–4	Perennial; useful between paving blocks.
SANTOLINA	E	3,4	Attractive foliage; use on banks.
SASA veitchii	E	2–4	Oriental, tropical effect.
SEDUM		1–4	Perennial; succulent used in rock gardens, borders, containers.
VINCA	E	1–4	Invasive; good on rough slopes.

VINES

Name of Plant	Evergreen or Deciduous	Climate Zones	Remarks
ANTIGONON leptopus	D,E	4	Fast growing; tolerates heat, needs winter protection; use on patios, terraces, fences, walls.
BEAUMONTIA grandiflora	E	4	High climbing, flowering; good for trellises, eaves.
CAMPSIS	D	1–4	Flowering, invasive; clings to wood, brick, stucco.
CISSUS	E	4	Use for trellises, walls, banks; controls erosion.
CLEMATIS	D	1–4	Attractive flowers; climbs trellises, trees.
EUONYMUS fortunei	E	1–4	Dense; good for shaded walls, fences, or as ground cover.
FATSHEDERA lizei	E	3,4	Good for espaliers, ground cover; needs strong support.
HEDERA	E	2–4	Plant near walls, fences, trellises; controls erosion as ground cover.
HYDRANGEA anomala	D	1–3	Flowering vine for shade.
POLYGONUM aubertii	D,E	1–4	Fast growing; good for screens, fences, arbors, hillsides.
SOLANDRA maxima	E	4	Grows well on walls, arbors, eaves.
TETRASTIGMA voinieranum	E	4	Fast growing; good for screens, eaves, lattices.
WISTERIA	D	1–4	Adaptable; attractive flowers.

LOW SHRUBS (3–6 feet)

Name of Plant	Evergreen or Deciduous	Climate Zones	Remarks
ABELIA (dwarf forms)	E	2–4	Use for borders, space dividers, banks.
CAMELLIA sasanqua	E	3,4	Good for espaliers, hedges, containers.
CHAMAECYPARIS	E	1–4	Needs fast drainage; use for containers, rock gardens, hedges.
CISTUS	E	3,4	Good plant for hot, dry banks.
EUONYMUS alata 'Compacta'	D	1–4	Background plant for screens, hedges.
JUNIPERUS	E	1–4	Use for screens, windbreaks, borders.
MYRSINE africana	E	3,4	Rounded form; good for hedges, backgrounds, foundations, narrow beds.
PHILODENDRON selloum	E	3,4	Tropical jungle effect; plant against walls, glass, or in pots.
PHOENIX roebelenii	E	4	Use in containers in sheltered locations.
PINUS mugo	E	1–4	Variable growth, from low to pyramidal tree of moderate size.
PINUS mugo mugo	E	1–4	Excellent container plant; good in rock gardens.
PITTOSPORUM tobira ''Wheeler's Dwarf''	E	3,4	Good for foregrounds or low boundaries, even small-scale ground cover.
PODOCARPUS macrophyllus	E	3	Plant in tubs or as screens, topiaries, hedges; will espalier.
PODOCARPUS nivalis	E	4	Dense; attractive as ground cover or in rock gardens.
RAPHIOLEPIS	E	4	Good for backgrounds, ground cover, dividers, informal hedges.
TAXUS cuspidata 'Nana'	E	1–4	Use for hedges, screens; plant grouped, single, or potted.
VIBURNUM burkwoodii 'Chenault'	D	1 4	Fragrant flowers; will espalier.

TALL SHRUBS (6 feet and over)

Name of Plant	Evergreen or Deciduous	Climate Zones	Remarks
ABELIA grandiflora	D,E	2–4	Good for borders, dividers, screens.
CAMELLIA	E	3,4	Use in containers or for espaliers, hedges, screens, ground cover.
EUONYMUS alata	D	1–4	Dense, flat-topped appearance; use for backgrounds, screens.
EUONYMUS japonica	E	1–4	Heat tolerant; group as hedge or screen.
EUONYMUS kiautschovica	E	1–4	Showy fruit; hardy to cold.
FATSIA japonica	E	3,4	Tropical appearance; shade loving.
GRISELINIA	E	4	Well-groomed appearance; use for screens, windbreaks.
JUNIPERUS	E	1–4	Pyramidal form; good for screens, windbreaks.
NANDINA domestica	E	2–4	Delicate foliage with flowers, fruit; use for hedges, screens.
PITTOSPORUM tobira	E	3,4	Use for screens, backgrounds.
PODOCARPUS macrophyllus	E	3,4	Good for screens, hedges, backgrounds.
XYLOSMA congestum	D,E	4	Handsome, versatile, graceful spreader; easily trained as espalier.
YUCCA	E	1–4	Tough, sword-shaped leaves; keep away from traffic areas

TREES

Name of Plant	Evergreen or Deciduous	Climate Zones	Remarks
ACER buergeranum	D	1–3	Low-spreading maple; good for patios.
ACER davidii	D	1–3	Handsome, upright maple; use on patios, lawns.
CHAMAECYPARIS obtusa	E	1–3	Plant in containers; use at entryways.
CHAMAEROPS humilis	E	3,4	Mass for hedges or use in containers.
CORDYLINE	E	4	Often sold as *Dracaena;* good for tropical backgrounds, containers.
CORNUS florida	D	1–3	Eastern dogwood; spring flowers.
CUPANIOPSIS anacardioides	E	4	Clean, handsome appearance; use on patios, lawns.
DRACAENA	E	4	Dramatic, palmlike silhouette; good in containers on patios.
ENSETE		3,4	Perennial; palmlike appearance; plant in containers and protect in winter.
EUCALYPTUS gunnii	E	3,4	Good for shade, windbreaks, screens.
FICUS lyrata	E	4	Dramatic form; needs protected location.
GINKGO biloba	D	1	Autumn color; leaves drop all at once.
JUNIPERUS	E	1–4	Dense, columnar form; good for screens, windbreaks.
LIVISTONA	E	4	Oriental appearance; slow growing.
MAGNOLIA grandiflora	E	1–4	Good for lawns, trees, espaliers, containers.
MAGNOLIA quinquepeta	D	1–4	Strong vertical effect; attractive flowers.
MUSA		3,4	Perennial; tender, needs protected location.
PINUS	E	1–4	Good for large rock gardens, containers.
SCHEFFLERA	E	4	Use for tropical effect.
STENOCARPUS sinuatus	E	3,4	Dense foliage, showy flowers; use on patios, terraces, lawns.
STRELITZIA nicolai	E	4	Litter-free; withstands splashing.

example. If you want to use them, plant them on the side of the pool away from the wind or where they're best sheltered from wind, to prevent litter from blowing into the water.

As in any garden setting, choose the right plant for the particular location. In small gardens where the pool and its pavement occupy almost all of the garden, container gardening comes into its own. Where a baffle fence is used for privacy or wind protection, or where the pool is enclosed with a wire fence for safety reasons, these structures offer an opportunity for interesting vine plantings.

Where there's an existing woodland setting, let the pool take the place of a small lake in a mountain meadow—a situation that neither requires nor benefits from a lot of additional planting.

When selecting flowering plants, aim for good design with beauty—if not bloom—the year around. Remember that in some areas early spring flowering varieties may bloom long before the

pool is in maximum use. Plants that bloom during the summer months when the pool is being used will brighten tubs, boxes, or insets in the pavement.

Fencing your pool

Enclosing a pool with a fence is good pool insurance. It keeps children, pets, and nonswimmers out of the pool when it's not in use and also provides security and privacy when you're swimming.

Indeed, many communities require fences with self-closing and self-latching gates around swimming pools. Check your local building department early in the landscape planning stages. Even if there's no code to this effect in your area, a fence is a good safety measure for your own children and those of your guests—even for nonswimming adults.

Besides providing a safe environment, fencing can be used to separate your lot from your neighbor's, to designate space, to conceal pool support equipment, and

even to store hanging pool maintenance equipment. A fence near the pool can keep debris from blowing into the pool and reduce maintenance. It also provides more specific climate control in your pool area; you can orient the fence panels to block out cool winds and admit sun when you want it.

Under no circumstances can safety or property line fencing be less than 3 feet from the edge of the pool; that's the minimum width required to permit safe passage around the pool.

The type of fence you build will be dictated by cost, location, the architectural style of your home, and the visual effect you want to achieve.

Whether you purchase a prefabricated kit, build the fence yourself from scratch, or have a professional do it, you'll find that advice from a landscape architect or fence contractor can help you decide what style and type of fence are best suited visually and functionally to your pool landscape (see illustrations below).

POOLSIDE FENCES

Open board

Louver

Wire mesh

Grapestake

Basket weave

Board

Solid panel

Fencing materials include wood, chain link, wire mesh, and wrought iron. For pool fences, choose pressure-treated wood or rust-resistant and noncorrosive metals.

The style of your fence can affect the amount of wind protection you receive in the pool area. For example, wind rushes over a solid fence like a stream of water. Such a fence provides little or no wind protection past the distance equal to its height.

Angling a baffle 45° into the wind extends maximum wind protection to a distance almost more than twice the fence height. Or, you can eliminate the downward crash of wind by using a baffle angled 45° with the wind. You'll feel warmest in the pocket below the baffle and at a distance equal to a little more than the fence height.

To break the wind flow, use fencing with openings at least ½ inch wide, or use plant screens. Up close, this type of fencing offers little protection; temperatures are warmest at a distance equal to twice the fence height. Dense plants offer even more protection.

Screens

Screens may be lightweight partitions made from bamboo or reed, canvas, wood, safety glass, or translucent plastic; or they may be living screens composed of plants and trees. Either way, they help control unwanted sun and wind,

POOLSIDE SCREENS

Reed

Plastic

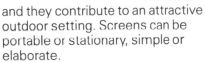
Glass

Wood

and they contribute to an attractive outdoor setting. Screens can be portable or stationary, simple or elaborate.

You can position screens to block the sun's heat and glare, the wind's chill, and the view of neighbors. Screens can also function to define space for showering and

dressing, lounging, and entertaining. Trailing, climbing, or espalier-type plants grow well on such screens.

Masonry walls

Masonry walls—constructed from concrete block, brick, stone, adobe,

POOLSIDE WALLS

Brick

Adobe

Stone

or poured concrete—are, for the most part, solid, sturdy, permanent, and practically maintenance-free.

Masonry walls are excellent barriers to sun, noise, and intruders. Because they store and reflect heat, masonry walls can heat or cool the area directly around them. Low masonry walls are also effective retaining walls for raised plants, beds, terraces, or embankments.

Masonry walls do have two major drawbacks: high cost and a tendency to give a closed-in feeling. You can cut costs by tackling some of the construction yourself. To make the area feel more inviting, build the wall only the minimum height required by code and at a distance from the pool. Arches, wrought iron panels, gates, or grilles created with bricks or concrete blocks can be incorporated in the wall to open up the space.

Plants can soften the lines and texture of masonry walls; the wall itself provides excellent support for climbing plants. But since masonry both absorbs and reflects heat, delicate plants may not fare well near a sunny wall.

Decks & pavement

The deck around the pool and any paved surfaces such as walks, patios, or steps are functional and versatile landscaping tools. They add usable space, provide a transition from one area to another, allow for drainage, and cover up barren soil.

Decks. Most pools are surrounded by a symmetrical or freeform deck. Besides creating a frame for the pool, the deck provides a safe walkway around the edge of the pool, and, if enlarged, provides space for pool furniture, a diving board, and lounging (see page 16).

In choosing a decking material, remember that the deck must be safe underfoot and not slippery, coarse, or uneven; using a heat-reflective material will keep the deck surface cooler. To prevent pool, hose, or rain water from entering the pool, the deck should drain away from the pool's coping.

POOLSIDE DECKING & PAVEMENT

Brick

Pavement block

Flagstone

Tile

Be sure the deck is easy to clean or hose down—it forms the barrier between the pool and your plants and will catch falling leaves, grass clippings, and other debris.

Choose a decking material that blends with or matches other paved areas and is resistant to acid, algae, bacteria, chemicals, frost, and funguses.

Brick, flagstone, tile, pavement block, and finished, colored, and exposed aggregate concrete are excellent decking materials. Other interesting decking materials are wood, outdoor carpeting, and cool-type concrete decking for hot climates.

Pavement. Paved surfaces in the pool area include patios, walks, low-level decks, steps, and special activity areas.

A patio can function as an entertainment or lounging area, as well as a transition between the house and pool. Walks permit passage from one area to another, provide a border for plantings, and can break up the straight lines of an angular lot. Low-level decks add more surface space on problem grade sites such as hillsides. Steps not only link one level to another, but also separate areas and levels.

Brick, concrete (finished, colored, or exposed aggregate), tile, flagstone, adobe blocks (use only the type with a burnt finish), and wood are durable and reliable pavement materials you can use in the pool landscape. Again, consider surface texture and color, ease of maintenance, weather resistance, and drainage capability.

Poolside structures

Chances are you won't want pool traffic in and out of your house, you'll need storage space for pool equipment, and you'll want to be outside by the pool as much as possible. The answer to it all is to build a structure near your pool—a pool house or cabana, a storage facility, a sauna, a gazebo, or some other enclosed or semi-enclosed area. Such a structure will add immeasurably to the comfort and attractiveness of your pool landscape.

Though your house and poolside structure can differ in style, their scale, texture, and material should be compatible. Remember that your structure must conform to local building codes, and you must have a building permit.

Shade structures.

Adding a shade structure such as a gazebo, patio roof, horizontal screen, or overhang makes for a more versatile pool environment. It can become a sheltered play area for children, a shady spot for relaxation and reading, and a place for eating and outdoor entertaining.

Gazebo, fine for entertaining, has storage and dressing rooms in rear.

Pool house.

A pool house can be simply a place to change in privacy and hang wet towels and bathing suits. Or it can be a shade more elaborate and include a shower and lavatory. Some pool houses are a lot more elaborate, designed as

warm-weather retreats complete with sauna, living and sleeping areas, and storage space.

A simpler approach is to incorporate a dressing room into your garage by erecting a few panels in a corner.

Pool house has room for shower and bath, sauna, changing area, and small kitchen.

Saunas.

A Finnish sauna and a swimming pool are a perfect match. After relaxing those tired

SHADE STRUCTURES

Egg crate

Woven canvas

Louver

Built-up roof

Reed

or tense muscles in the hot sauna, you'll find a plunge in the pool feels totally invigorating.

Your sauna can be a freestanding structure in a private, unused corner of your yard near the pool, or it can be incorporated into your pool house. You can purchase saunas in kits, either prefabricated or precut, or custom-made.

Storage structures. You'll need considerable storage space for the support system, vacuum, leaf skimmer, brushes, and chemicals. You'll probably also need space to store poolside furniture, game equipment, and other accessories during off seasons.

Sheltering pool support equipment in a well-ventilated, covered area prolongs their life. If the support equipment is installed near a fence, garage, house wall, or garden storage shed, only a simple windscreen or fence extension with a lean-to roof is required.

Small building, an extension of brick wall, shelters support equipment.

Long-handled cleaning equipment can be hung neatly on hooks in a wall or fence. Just be sure they don't block access to the pool support equipment. Keep chlorine and other pool chemicals locked in a cool, dry, dark place.

Protect pool or patio furniture, game equipment, and other pool accessories from the elements by storing them in the garage, in storage boxes that double as benches, or in utility storage areas.

Lighting the pool landscape

As an area to view and a background for entertaining, a swimming pool offers almost as much pleasure as in the swimming it provides. At night, with tastefully arranged outdoor lighting, the view of your pool and landscaping can be especially appealing.

A first concern in lighting a swimming pool is the safety and level of illumination within the pool—the underwater lighting. In most pools, there's a light at the deep end of the pool several feet below the diving board. If the pool has been located with the deep end nearest the house, the glare from the underwater light occasioned by waves and splashing is directed away from the house. But if glare is directed toward the house, you can install a dimmer in the lighting circuit. A dim glow of light is all that's necessary to identify the edge of the pool and provide a soft background for parties, cocktail hours, and late evening swimming. Use full brilliance when children are swimming.

When installing lighting in the landscaping around the pool, arrange the lights to reflect the pool's surface. With the underwater lights off, the shimmering water will make an especially attractive setting, even when viewed from inside the house.

If you're designing your own outdoor lighting, experiment with lights in various locations. Buy several inexpensive clamp-on lights and reflectors and some long extension cords. Place them in the areas you want to light and observe the results at night. If you're not satisfied, move the lights around until you get the effect you want.

If you're installing the lighting system yourself, you'll want to consult the *Sunset* book *Basic Wiring Illustrated* for information on both 110-volt and 12-volt lighting.

Getting the work done

Will your pool landscaping be a do-it-yourself project, a professional project, or a combination of both?

The do-it-yourselfer. There are several ways you can approach the design and development of your pool landscape providing you have the experience, time, skill, and energy.

You can create the landscape design and then carry it out yourself, or you can design it and hire a contractor to do the actual work. You can even work on parts of the project you're capable of doing yourself and hire subcontractors with the skills you don't have—gardening, electrical wiring, paving, or excavation.

No matter how you chose to do the work, you'll benefit from consulting professional at some point, preferably during the design stage. A professional can offer sound design and construction advice and make sure that your landscape design conforms to the local building regulations.

Professionals. With a project as enormous and involved as developing or remodeling a pool landscape, you may find it best to rely totally on professionals—architects, landscape architects, landscape designers, contractors, nurserymen, or gardeners.

Putting your ideas on paper

Whether you're designing the landscaping yourself or retaining a professional to do it for you, you'll want to draw up some plans based on your own ideas first. If you've already made a plot plan to determine your pool location, you can use that for your landscape design. If not, you'll want to make one (see page 9).

Use tracing paper laid over the plot plan to sketch the various approaches. Plan for what you'd most like to have, then count the costs. Creating a strong design will help you distinguish between the more important and less important elements of your plan.

Try to think in three dimensions to help you balance the design elements and visualize the results. And remember, changing your plans on paper costs nothing.

TREATING YOUR POOL WATER

Filtration, chemical treatment, and cleaning (see page 109) are the three essential methods of keeping your pool water clear, clean, and free of bacteria. Beginning from the time the pool is filled, the job of maintaining safe pool water continues the year around for the life of the pool.

You can hire a pool service company to do the job, or do the work yourself. During the summer, you'll have to spend 4 to 8 hours a week treating the water. Winter chores take far less time if the pool is not in use and may be almost nonexistent if you keep the pool covered. You can minimize your work by installing automatic devices for chemical treatment and pool vacuuming (see page 89).

This chapter covers filtering the water, chemically treating it, and filling the pool.

THE ROLE OF FILTRATION

The filtration system (see page 22) is the primary method for removing solid material that clouds the water; it also disperses the pool chemicals throughout the water so they can do their job (see below).

A properly designed system should pass *all* the water in the pool through the filter within a given period of time, usually 8 hours. This is called the turnover rate. Without proper circulation the pool will have dead areas where the water stagnates and is never or seldom filtered, even though the filter may be working perfectly.

The filtration system serves another purpose—it moves hot water from the heater and disperses it throughout the pool. The pump in the filtration system should turn on before the heater comes on. The pump should stay on until after the heater shuts off to remove the hot water from the heater and pipes and prevent mineral deposits from building up in the pipes.

Never run the filtration system less than 4 to 5 hours during the summer and 2 to 3 hours during the winter months. Keep the system running when the temperatures are below freezing to prevent ice from forming in the system. When a lot of people are using the pool, you'll need to increase the filtering time to keep the water clear. At these times, turn the system on and off manually rather than resetting the time clock.

With reduced filtration times, be sure to always maintain adequate disinfectant residuals. Whenever poor water clarity or chemical imbalance become apparent, increase the filtration time in half hour increments until the condition is corrected.

After filling the pool for the first time, you'll need to run the filter continuously until the water is clear. In properly filtered and chemically treated water, you can clearly see the main drain in the deep end of the pool.

To conserve energy, you'll want to determine the minimum amount of filtration time required to obtain good water clarity. To do this, start with a daily filtration that's the same as the turnover rate (see above), usually 8 hours. If, after several days, the water is still unclouded, gradually reduce the time in half hour steps until you reach the minimum amount of time needed to maintain water clarity. If 8 hours does not keep the water clear, increase the time in half hour increments.

Controlling filtration

Perhaps the smallest expenditure you can make for your pool for the greatest convenience is a time clock. Once you determine the filtration schedule, you can set the time clock and allow it to turn the pump on and off for you. Some time clocks will even reduce the time during the week and lengthen it on weekends if that's when the pool load is heaviest. You can also use a clock to turn the heater on and off.

POOL WATER CHEMISTRY

Treating your pool water with chemicals maintains the chemical balance, disinfects the water, and keeps it sparkling clear.

It's not hard to do this job yourself—you'll need to test the water regularly for various characteristics and then add the correct amounts of certain chemicals, if required. Because the formulation of chemicals varies between manufacturers, follow the instructions on the container. Many pool service and supply companies will test your water and advise you of any needed chemical changes without charge to you.

How to test your pool water

Proper water testing is your major guarantee against the development of serious problems. Consider test kits a guide to the well-being of your pool; they provide the information necessary to determine the chemical requirements of the water.

A basic test kit will enable you to test for pH and disinfectant residual. Other kits include these as well as tests for total alkalinity, combined and total disinfectant, alkali demand, and acid demand. Individual kits for testing levels of cyanuric acid and calcium hardness are also available.

Pool water test kit contains vials, test reagents, and instructions.

Testing is a simple process—you fill a small tube with pool water and add a reagent in the form of a tablet or a few drops of test solution. The treated water is then compared to either color standards or calculations provided with the kit.

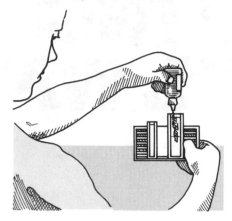

Pool water is tested by adding reagent to water in vial and comparing color to scale.

The best time to test the water is in the early evening. Avoid surface water when you fill the tube; take a sample from a depth of at least 12 inches. When you add the specified amount of reagent mix gently but don't place your thumb over the top of the tube—body acid can affect the reading. Look at the color against a light (preferably white) background—but not against the sun—and read the test within 4 to 5 seconds after adding the reagent. Always rinse the tube after use, and never use it for any other type of solution.

Water balance

Acidity, alkalinity, and the amount of mineral salts in the water must be kept in balance to prevent corrosion of metal parts, scale deposits, and etching of plaster surfaces. Proper balance also helps to reduce the need for sanitizing agents, allowing these chemicals to do their work effectively.

All water has an acid-alkaline balance that's measured on a pH scale. The scale runs from 0 to 14 with the center, 7, indicating a neutral state. Numbers above 7 represent varying degrees of alkalinity; lower values stand for degrees of acidity. For example, muriatic acid has a pH of about 0, vinegar is 3, distilled water is 7, and lye solutions are close to 14.

Controlling the chemical balance of pool water is vital. The ideal range is slightly on the alkaline side, between 7.4 and 7.6 on the pH scale. If the pH is too high (alkaline), disinfectants are less effective in destroying bacteria and algae; water will be cloudy, scale can develop on heater coils and plaster surfaces, and the filter can be blocked. If the pH is too low (acidic), it will cause eye and skin irritation, corrosion of metal parts, and etching and discoloration of plaster. Because overacidity can be the most serious, do not allow the pH to get below 7.2. When the pH is below 7.2 or above 7.6, eyes will burn or smart.

Testing pH is not difficult. The water sample in the test kit will change color according to the pH. For example, a phenol red indicator will turn the sample yellow for acid, orange for little or no alkali, and red for high alkalinity. A good test kit should have at least 4 color gradations between 7.2 and 8.0 so you can get an accurate reading.

During the summer months, the pH should be tested three times a week. In the winter, after initial water balance, once a week or even less should be sufficient. Always test for pH after a storm or at other times when large quantities of contaminants have been carried into the water.

Total alkalinity and pH. Total alkalinity refers to the amount and type (in ppm—parts per million parts of water by weight) of all the alkali soluble salts in the water. To change the level and type of alkali salts, you must change the amount.

The water used in many pools is high in alkalinity, creating problems in adjusting the pH. Though pH is quickly controlled by chemicals, it can bounce around on the scale daily or even hourly; this fluctuation can be considerably lessened by adjusting the total alkalinity in a plastered pool to within an 80 to 120 ppm range. The range for a vinyl-lined, painted, or fiberglass pool is 125 to 150 ppm.

Total alkalinity can be very different in different pools because of varying programs of water treatment, water sources, and the amount of fresh water added to the pool. If your pool's alkalinity is high and the pH is over 7.8, add enough acid (a little at a time) to bring the pH down to 7.4. The pH will probably rise again, so continue the treatment until the water tests out consistently at 7.4 to 7.6 over a period of a few days. Each time you add acid the amount should be enough to drop the total alkalinity by about 6 to 12 ppm.

As the total alkalinity level approaches the correct range, the pH should be checked often to make sure it does not drop below 7.2 at any time. Once the total alkalinity level has been reached, the pH will be buffered to a point where further acid control will be minimal.

Total alkalinity is tested much like pH. After the first adjustment of total alkalinity, it needs to be sampled only about once a month. An acid test kit is available to tell you just how much acid to use, but whether you use the test kit or just add acid until your pH tester shows the right balance, it's advisable to add only small amounts at a time for best control.

Add chemicals to your pool only in the evening or early morning; keep the filtration system operating for at least an hour afterwards to ensure proper mixing. The best place to add acid is in the deep end of the pool, about 1½ feet away from the wall and in an area clear of air suction or return lines. Follow the manufacturer's instructions in adding acid to the pool.

Chemicals for raising pH. Sodium carbonate (soda ash) is an inexpensive, effective, quick-acting pH adjuster. Half-pound cakes of soda ash can be suspended in pool water and will dissolve in about 3 to 4 hours. To use the chemical in granular form, walk around the pool and sprinkle it into the water. It can also be premixed with water; for the average residential pool dissolve one pound in hot water and pour it into the pool as you walk around the perimeter. Wait for one hour (with filter operating) and take a pH reading. If necessary, repeat until the pH has reached the proper level.

Chemicals for raising alkalinity. Sodium bicarbonate (common baking soda) is inexpensive and easy to use but only half as strong as soda ash. Use as needed to increase total alkalinity and pH. One and a half pounds raises alkalinity 10 ppm for every 10,000 gallons of water.

Chemicals for lowering pH and alkalinity. Muriatic acid (liquid) is the most popular pH and alkalinity adjuster. It stores well, and small amounts can change pH significantly. However, if incorrectly applied it can be very damaging. One pint for every 5000 gallons of water reduces alkalinity quickly. Add no more than one pint per 10,000 gallons of water at a time and wait for one hour before adding more acid. Handle it carefully to prevent splashing yourself, and wash off any spillage immediately. Do not add muriatic acid through the skimmer.

Sodium bisulphate (dry acid) is the most readily available dry acid for pH adjustment. It's easier to store than liquids and is good for small pools that require small quantities. To use it, dissolve the acid in water and spread it around the pool. Follow the instructions on the label for proper amounts. It should be premixed with water (always add acid to water, never water to acid). Handle it carefully.

Disinfecting the pool water

Bacteria are the main cause of unsanitary pool water. These microscopic organisms, some of them harmful, invade pool water by means of carriers—mostly people. Particularly in smaller pools with heavy use—including children's wading pools—bacteria control cannot be overemphasized.

Methods used in industry and in scientific laboratories to disinfect or sterilize water are gradually being adopted for residential swimming pool use. Such methods include electrolytic chlorine generation, ultraviolet sterilization, ozone oxidation, and reverse osmosis.

Iodine and bromine have met with intermittent success as disinfectants but are used in few residential pools. Chlorine is by far the most popular disinfecting agent. It is available as gas, liquid, powder, and tablet and has proven to be effective and easy to use. Check the package to be sure the chemical has been registered with the Environmental Protection Agency for swimming pool use.

The use of chlorine. Chlorine gas is generally restricted to public pools. Contained in a pressure tank, the gas requires special handling and an automatic feeder. Liquid chlorine (sodium hypochlorite) and dry chlorine (calcium hypochlorite and chlorinated isocyanurates) are the major types used in residential swimming pools.

Automatic chlorinators and hypochlorinators of erosion and solution types dispense the proper amount of disinfectant in the water. They are easily installed, either with a new filtering system or at a later date. Operating continuously during the filtering cycle, chlorinators regulate the amount of chlorine added to the water in accordance with the pool's requirements. As a result, the pool is kept sanitary at all times and may be left unattended for long periods.

Though the automatic feeder releases you from hand-feeding your pool, you still need to use your test kit regularly to keep tabs on the sanitary condition and chemical balance of the water.

If your pool is not equipped with an automatic chlorinator, add chlorine only in the evening or early morning hours. Keep the filtration system on to distribute the chlorine in the pool.

Chlorine residual. Whenever you add chlorine, it immediately goes to work killing algae and bacteria, but in the process some of it is destroyed by these same algae and bacteria. The amount of chlorine used up in this manner is the chlorine demand of the water. The amount of disinfectant left in the water is referred to as the chlorine residual. This free residual keeps the pool sanitary, and only a small amount of it is required.

Pool water also contains ammonia and other compounds of nitrogen, particularly ammonia nitrogen. Nitrogenous compounds, in the form of human wastes in the water and fertilizers used near the pool, are the primary sources. Chlorine and ammonia combine to form chloramines, which cause burning eyes, skin irritation, and the unpleasant odor often associated with chlorine, particularly pungent if the pH is low. If you can smell the chlorine, there isn't enough residual chlorine in the water, as chlorine in an uncombined state is practically odorless.

The chlorine residual, that which is not combined with nitrogen, should never drop below 1.0 ppm; it can range up to 3.0 ppm or even a little higher, but 1.0 ppm is ideal. Chlorine residual is tested much the same way as pH. Follow the instructions in your test kit.

Sunlight, water temperature, heavy pool use, and wind can all deplete the chlorine residual. Regular use of chlorinated isocyanurate—2 or 3 times a week during the summer—should keep the residual at a safe level. But a day of heavy use can destroy all the chlorine in the water unless you take preventive measures by adding an extra dose before swimmers arrive. Even then, the supply may have to be replenished at the end of the day to restore the residual level, unless the water is conditioned.

Superchlorination. Superchlorination involves adding 5 to 7 times the normal dose of chlorine (usually in the form of unstabilized chlorine) to pool water to burn out nitrogen compounds and human wastes. This is generally accomplished by the direct manual addition of a gallon of liquid or a pound of dry chlorine to each 10,000 gallons of pool water.

You'll want to superchlorinate either when the combined chlorine reading is higher than 0.2 ppm, or about every 2 weeks during the swimming season, whichever comes first.

Superchlorination should be done only after sundown, since the ultraviolet sun rays are likely to destroy some of the chemical. Close the pool to swimmers until the residual level drops to normal, 1.0 to 3.0 ppm free chlorine.

Conditioning the pool. The major disadvantage of chlorine is its tendency to dissipate in sunlight. Many pool owners use cyanuric acid or a combination of chlorine and cyanuric acid, to filter out ultraviolet sun rays, permitting the chlorine to do its job of disinfecting.

The swimming pool usually is conditioned to about 40 ppm of cyanuric acid when the pool is first filled, and additional application is needed only as splashout and backwashing require water to be added if you're not using chlorinated isocyanurate. Though conditioning of the pool requires a special test kit and adds to the initial cost of chemicals, expenditure is usually compensated for by the long-term effects on the chlorine residual and the reduced need of acid for pH adjustment.

Though referred to as an acid, cyanuric acid has very low toxicity and little effect on pH. According

PROPER USE OF CHEMICALS

Because swimming pool maintenance involves chemicals that can be harmful if not handled properly, it is very important to follow certain procedures in using them.

• Never use someone else's pool water test results or filtration procedures as a guide for your own pool.

• Never mix any pool chemicals together unless so directed by the manufacturer on the label of the container. Common household bleaches, if used to clean pool areas, must never be mixed with or used simultaneously with household drain cleaners— the combination will form poisonous chlorine gas.

• Keep all pool chemicals and cleaning agents sealed, and store them in a locked, dry area out of reach of children; the key should be available only to adults familiar with the use of the chemicals.

• Do not store chemicals in enclosed support system rooms, since even covered containers can emit corrosive fumes that can damage the support system.

• Add chemicals to water carefully. Hold a container of liquid close to the surface of the water so the chemical won't splash on skin or clothes; sprinkle granulated products close to the water surface so they won't be blown.

• Wash your hands with soap and water after using chemicals.

• Handle all acids with extreme care. Follow the manufacturers' directions carefully.

• Always read the labels of chemicals, both when you buy them and when you use them. Labels sometimes look similar; adding the wrong chemical can lead to harmful conditions.

• Use only those sanitizing agents and algaecides registered with the Environmental Protection Agency for pool or spa use. The package should carry an EPA registration number.

to the U.S. Public Health Service, concentrations of up to 100 ppm are safe.

Sanitizing agents. Liquid chlorine (sodium hypochlorite) is an in-inexpensive chlorine form. It disperses quickly in water and leaves no residue to add to water hardness. It has a lower chlorine content than dry forms and requires careful handling to avoid splashing, damage to clothes, and possible fading of colors in pool finishes. If stored too long, liquid chlorine can deteriorate. Liquid chlorine raises the total alkalinity and pH of pool water.

Add liquid chlorine and acid to pool so as to avoid splashing.

Dry chlorine (calcium hypochlorite) is available in granulated or tablet form. It is inexpensive and stores well but disperses more slowly than liquid chlorine. It contains about 65 percent available chlorine.

Add dry chlorine around edge of pool.

The granulated type may be added directly to the pool and is particularly good for spot treatments of clinging algae. But it leaves a calcium residue that can clog D.E. filters, turn the water milky, and sometimes cause the grains of sand in sand filters to cement. To prevent this, combine 8 ounces of powder with 10 quarts of water in a nonmetallic container. Stir for at least 30 seconds, then set aside out of the sun for 30 minutes to allow the solids to settle. Pour the clear liquid into the pool, and discard the sediment.

Tablets are suspended in baskets near the inlet lines in the pool. Chlorine is released gradually as the flow of incoming water dissolves the tablets. You can also put the tablets in a floating container and let them dissolve slowly in the water as the floater drifts around the pool. When using either of these methods, be sure to check the chlorine level frequently; chlorine is being dispensed even when the pump isn't running.

Dry chlorine, like liquid chlorine, raises the alkalinity and pH of the pool water.

Chlorinated isocyanurates are chlorine compounds with cyanuric acid base. After a pool has been initially conditioned with cyanuric acid, this form of chlorine will automatically replace the conditioner lost through splashout and backwash. These chlorine compounds are easy to use, dissolve readily, leave no calcium residue to damage filter media, and do not appreciably alter the pH. They're available in tablets, sticks, or granulated form.

Continued use of chlorinated isocyanurates may cause the cyanuric level in the water to increase over a period of years if water is not discarded by backwash or splashout. If the water tests out at over 100 ppm, the pool may have to be partially drained and refilled with fresh water. To forestall this, liquid chlorine or lithium or calcium hypochlorite should be used as a superchlorinator.

Elemental bromine is nearly equal to chlorine as a bactericide, but the extreme care required in

handling it has limited its use in residential pools. Organic bromine is available in stick form and can be used in the same manner as the hypochlorites and isocyanurates, but it is more costly. The sticks dissolve into the recirculating system from a pressure vessel controlling the rate the disinfectant is fed into the pool water. The stick form of bromine lowers the pH to the acidic side.

Iodine has been used to a limited degree. Though easy to use, it's less effective than chlorine and can turn the water green. Iodine is difficult to test for residual, and the water balance must be carefully controlled.

SPECIAL WATER PROBLEMS

You'll probably have at least one of the following problems from time to time. Some are inherent in the original water supply; others arise because of extreme weather conditions, temporary lapses in chemical treatment or filtration, or heavy pool use.

Algae

The regular use of an algaecide and good water maintenance normally will keep algae under control. If the water takes on a greenish or mustard-colored cast and black or dark green spots appear on the surface finish, you probably have algae.

There are two types of algae: free-floating and clinging. Some of the clinging varieties may resist all of your regular efforts and hang on as black, green, or brown patches on plaster finishes. There are several ways to get rid of an algae infestation.

• Check the total alkalinity of your pool. If it's not in the 80 to 120 ppm range, adjust it. Also adjust the pH to 7.2 to 7.4, then superchlorinate with as much as 2 gallons of liquid chlorine (or 2 pounds of calcium hypochlorite) for each 10,000 gallons of water. Shut down the filter for about 24 hours. Brush the walls briskly, restart the filter, and vacuum away dead algae. To get rid of black spots, brush the pool and turn the pump off. When the water becomes still, carefully pour trichlorinated isocyanurate into the pool so it covers the area. Brush again the next day. Then turn on the pump to filter out the debris. Do not allow swimmers in the pool during this period.

• Persistent colonies clinging to interior surfaces sometimes can be destroyed by pouring liquid chlorine right on top of them or by placing dry chlorine in a nylon stocking and using it as a scouring pad (wear rubber gloves). However, only the outer layers of cells may be killed, leaving surviving cells beneath to re-emerge when growth conditions are favorable.

• Many pool contractors and service companies recommend using an algaecide as a routine part of maintenance. Make sure the algaecide you select is effective against all strains of algae, and carefully follow instructions on the label. Ask your pool service for recommendations.

• Pool stones are available for grinding off spots of algae on plaster. Either dive down to a spot or attach the stone to the end of your brush pole and work from above. This treatment does not remove the roots of the algae.

• If algae persists, call in a professional service company for help. There are other, more complex algae treatments available, but it's better to rely on competent advice before adding strange chemicals to the water.

• Check the chlorine residual and pH after heavy chemical treatments, and do not allow swimmers in pool until the water is properly balanced and the chlorine is at a safe level.

Colored water

Color in a newly filled pool may result from algae or vegetation sources such as tannin; the color will bleach out when sufficient chlorine is added. Color is also caused by suspended dirt, which filtration will remove.

The most troublesome causes of coloration are minerals in the water. Many pools will fill perfectly clear but become reddish brown or black after standing exposed to the air or when chlorine is added. This is caused by a soluble form of iron or manganese which becomes insoluble when oxidized by oxygen or chlorine (see page 107).

Hazy or turbid water is too alkaline, lacks sufficient filtration time or chlorination, needs a water clarifying agent, or a combination. Green, green blue, or milky water indicates chemical imbalance, poor filtration, or both. If the balance is normal, the water may contain iron (see page 107).

With any colored water you'll need to filter almost continuously and test and adjust the water chemically until the condition is corrected.

Stains

A pool surface can be stained by debris, metal objects, algae, and mineral deposits. Yellow or reddish brown stains may be caused by iron in the fill water. Too much acid added to the water at one time can cause stains, and, if added too close to the surface skimmer, will be carried into the pipes and filtration system, causing corrosion particles to appear as stains. It also can corrode the piping, filter, and heating system. Maintain the proper pH to help prevent these problems.

Hairpins, toys, or other metal objects dropped into the pool should be removed immediately to prevent rust stains.

On a plaster finish, buffing ordinary stains with waterproof sandpaper may remove them. A dilute solution of muriatic acid (1 part acid to 10 parts water) also can be used, if great care is taken not to etch the surrounding plaster. Excess etching not only visually mars the surface, but the cracks and crevices become excellent breeding grounds for algae. On a painted pool, stains can be removed by scrubbing them with a strong detergent or chlorine solution.

Scale

Scale is caused mainly by an accumulation of calcium salts and usually appears first on heater coils. The heater should not be operated as long as these conditions exist. To correct them, add a chemical scale inhibitor to the pool water or adjust pH, calcium hardness, and total alkalinity to a proper balance.

Scale also will appear as a gray or brownish crust on tile or cement. Maintaining total alkalinity and hardness levels in balance helps control these deposits, but over time, evaporation causes most pools to develop increasingly higher mineral content. The water should be checked every year or two by a professional to make sure the mineral level does not get high enough to cause a serious scale problem.

Well-developed scale deposits usually cannot be removed with sandpaper or home remedies. The only alternative is to call in a professional to drain, power-sand, and acid-wash the pool.

Corrosion and electrolysis

Corrosion can result from an over-acidic condition, improper use of acid chemicals, or oxidation. Corrosion also can be caused by electrolysis. Whenever two different metals come in contact with chemically treated water, a small electrical current flows between the metals. This current does not give an electric shock, but it can cause corrosion of active metals such as iron and produce rust spots on metal.

FILLING A NEW POOL

Don't be surprised if the water in your new pool looks cloudy after the first filling. The suspended particles present in all drinking water are simply more evident in a large quantity of water, but a day or two of filtration along with disinfection will remove the cloudiness.

Vinyl-lined and fiberglass pools are usually filled at the same time as the pool shell is backfilled. Because inlets and skimmer openings must be cut in the vinyl liner as the water reaches each level of opening, filling the pool is intermittent. Other types of pools are filled continuously until the water line is reached.

A new pool with a plaster finish requires special attention during the first few weeks. It's important to fill it immediately and maintain a continuous flow to prevent dirt rings from forming and the plaster from cracking.

If copper tanks and pipes in the recirculation system are seriously corroded by electrolysis, the copper must be replaced. Though many pools are never troubled with electrolysis, it does happen often enough to warrant preventive measures. Check periodically for corrosion near valves where copper and iron, or other dissimilar metals, come together. In filter tanks, engineers may recommend using a sacrificial magnesium anode to draw the electrolytic deposit away from the tank.

Electrolysis can blacken chrome parts. Because the source of the electric current often is evasive, call in an engineering firm or pool company to diagnose the problem.

Filling the pool yourself

Most pool companies and contractors include initial filling and water treatment in your contract. If you're confronted with doing the task yourself, the following procedure is recommended.

• Test the source of the fill water. Use your test kit for pH and disinfectant, total alkalinity, and acid demand. This survey of the water's condition will give you a preliminary idea of the type and amount of chemicals needed to balance and disinfect the pool water. Also check and treat for iron and other metals.

• Fill the pool according to the contractor's instructions. For a pool with a plaster finish, your contractor or plasterer will tell you when to

begin filling and how to keep the stream of fresh water from gouging the finish. One way is to wrap and tie a bundle of burlap over the end of the hose. Place the end of the hose on the main drain and turn on the water. As the water gets deeper, you can raise the end of the hose and move it farther away from the plaster.

• Start the filter according to the manufacturer's instructions; add 1 gallon of liquid chlorine or 6 ounces of chlorinated isocyanurate for every 10,000 gallons of water in the pool. Also add an algaecide, following the manufacturer's instructions.

You'll need to keep dirt from collecting on the walls while the plaster is curing. Frequent brushing will help clean the dirt off, but do not use a vacuum cleaner during the first 2 weeks—the wheels can mar the surface. A fine, cloudy sediment of plaster dust will result from the brushing, but the filtration system will take care of most of the cloudiness.

Because the fine plaster dust will clog the filter media, backwash sand and D.E. filters frequently (see page 109). If your pool filter is equipped with cartridges, most pool builders will supply you with an extra set of cartridges. After the plaster dust is filtered out, it's easier to dispose of the first set than to attempt cleaning them off (see page 109). You can scoop out leaves and debris with a leaf skimmer (be careful not to mar the plaster). Do not let the pH fall below 7.4—acid water is very damaging to new plaster. Test for chlorine daily during this period and add chlorine as needed, but don't superchlorinate for about 2 weeks.

• Adjust the total alkalinity to within 80 to 120 ppm, adding acid according to the acid demand test kit. Also test for pH and adjust it to within 7.4 to 7.6. (Remember—do not mix any chemicals together, allow time for each addition to circulate thoroughly, and do not allow the pH to drop below 7.2.)

• Condition the pool water with cyanuric acid to 40 ppm if recommended by your pool builder or service company.

The presence of iron

In some areas, water used to fill the pool may contain iron. Iron causes a red tint, sometimes deepening to dark brown. Water containing iron should be treated as soon as the pool is filled; otherwise, it can stain a plaster pool and clog the filtration system.

If your water supply is from a municipal water company, such a condition is not likely, but if your source is an underground well not previously treated, test a sample before filling the pool. Fill a glass gallon jug with water from the source and add about ½ ounce liquid or dry chlorine; shake and let stand for an hour. If the water darkens, you have iron or manganese in the source water.

If the iron content is extensive and you have a plaster pool, ask your pool contractor or a service company for advice; removing iron without staining the plaster can be complex.

Chlorine will oxidize iron and precipitate it out of the solution into rust particles. If you add chlorine to the water to remove the iron, use only small amounts at a time. With each addition, some of the iron particles will settle to the bottom of the pool; vacuum them up immediately. Repeat the process until the pool water is clear.

Another method is to floc the pool with alum. When alum is dissolved in pool water, a form of aluminum hydroxide—called floc— is formed. With a sand filter you can floc the water with 1 pound of potassium alum per 5000 gallons of water. (Before adding the alum, be sure the pH is in the range of 7.6 to 8.0.) The gel-like floc traps the iron, preventing it from contacting the plaster. Diatomaceous earth filters will collect finer particles than sand, so continuous operation of the system for about 48 hours should clear the pool water. Alum can block diatomaceous earth, so vacuum the settled floc from the pool floor, taking care not to recirculate the water through the filtration system. Otherwise, you'll have to change the diatomaceous earth frequently.

PROTECTING YOUR INVESTMENT

Neglect of the pool shell, the pool equipment, or even the water itself can mar the appearance of the pool and ruin the interior finish and the support system in a surprisingly short time. Having invested so much in a pool, you'll want to protect it by accepting maintenance responsibilities as part of your life style.

Maintenance of your swimming pool begins as soon as you fill it with water and continues the year around. Summer and winter, your pool needs some attention to keep the equipment functioning smoothly, the water clean, and the pool shell in good condition.

Pool maintenance doesn't require a great deal of backbreaking labor but rather a regular schedule of routine work intended to make your pool pleasant to swim in and to ward off serious problems. In general, you can count on spending 4 to 8 hours a week working around the pool during the summer, if you do all the maintenance yourself. Winter chores will be far easier and may be practically nonexistent if you cover the pool during the coldest months.

In many areas, pool service companies will maintain and chemi-cally treat your pool. The monthly charge varies depending on the geographical area, the competition, the number of service calls, and the pool's size. Most companies will visit the pool two or three times a week during the swimming season and once a week or less during the off-season.

Maintenance procedures outlined here are based on a concrete pool with a plaster finish. If you have a vinyl-lined or fiberglass pool, maintenance of the interior surfaces will be easier, since the non-porous finishes resist algae growth, calcium deposits, and dirt accumulations. But water treatment (see page 101) is about the same in all pools regardless of their construction method or interior finish.

MAINTENANCE EQUIPMENT

Very few pieces of equipment are required to maintain a pool. A vacuum cleaner, leaf skimmer, and brushes are the basic units. Nothing more that you may obtain—and there's a wide variety of other accessories from which to choose—is really essential.

Vacuum cleaners

One type of vacuum cleaner works from a vacuum inlet that's part of the filtration system. The cleaner consists of a suction head, wheels for mobility, a nylon brush for removing stubborn dirt (this is not included in some models), a floating hose from the suction head to the vacuum fitting, and a handle.

The cleaner is hooked up to the vacuum fitting or to the skimmer if it has a vacuum connection and is pushed slowly around the bottom of the pool. Water, dirt, and debris are pulled into the filtration system. Leaves and other large objects, such as pieces of paper, are caught in the strainer basket; smaller particles are removed in the filter. The clear water is then returned to the pool through the inlets.

The second type of cleaner, called a jet cleaner, does not depend on the filtration system as its power source, so it's extremely useful in pools without vacuum fittings. Similar to a carpet sweeper, it can be quickly assembled and moved rapidly across the pool surfaces.

The jet cleaner uses a garden hose connected to a standard house faucet to create the vacuum action at the cleaner head. Water is forced through the hose into the throat of the suction head and up into a filter bag attached to the vacuum cleaner. The movement of water pulls dirt off the bottom of the pool as the cleaner is moved around. The refuse is pulled into the filter bag where it's caught, and the clean water passes right through the weave of the cotton or plastic cloth bag.

When the vacuuming is completed, the filter bag is removed and cleaned. Jet cleaners work rapidly and remove leaves much better than the standard vacuum cleaner and filter combination. On the other hand, the standard combination picks up fine debris much better than the jet cleaner.

Some pool owners, trying to get by without a vacuum cleaner, use a brush to push the dirt into the main drain. Though you save the initial cost of the vacuum cleaner, brushing can never do as complete a job as vacuuming.

Leaf skimmers

The leaf skimmer is simply an aluminum, stainless steel, or plastic frame with a plastic mesh skimming net. These units are available in a number of sizes and styles, including one with a scoop surface for removing large objects.

Brushes

If your pool is finished with paint, vinyl, or fiberglass, you need only one brush for general cleaning of walls and floor. Nylon bristles are usually recommended for long life. If your pool has a plaster finish, you'll also need a stainless steel brush for removing algae, rust stains, and entrenched dirt.

Handles

Aluminum handles that fit the vacuum cleaner, leaf skimmer, and brushes are available in lengths ranging from 8 to 16 feet. One handle is enough for most pool owners, since it can be used interchangeably with all the cleaning tools. Telescopic handles are helpful if trees or structures close to the water limit maneuverability.

Automatic pool cleaners

An automatic pool cleaner saves considerable time and effort by eliminating the need to vacuum and, in some cases, the need to brush. If you're using a pool service company, an automatic system may even reduce your monthly fee.

Some types of automatic pool cleaners can be installed at any time; others must be built in when your pool is under construction. For information on the various types of automatic cleaners, see the special feature, "Pool Accessories," on page 88.

REGULAR CLEANING PROCEDURE

There's no set pattern for pool clean-up; you work out a procedure that best suits your particular situation. But the National Pool and Spa Institute recommends an eight-step maintenance procedure that's followed by many pool service firms and will serve as a good starting point for new pool owners.

1. Use the leaf skimmer to collect debris floating on the surface of the pool or lying on the bottom. It's much easier to skim the surface than dredge the bottom, so use the

CLEANING TOOLS

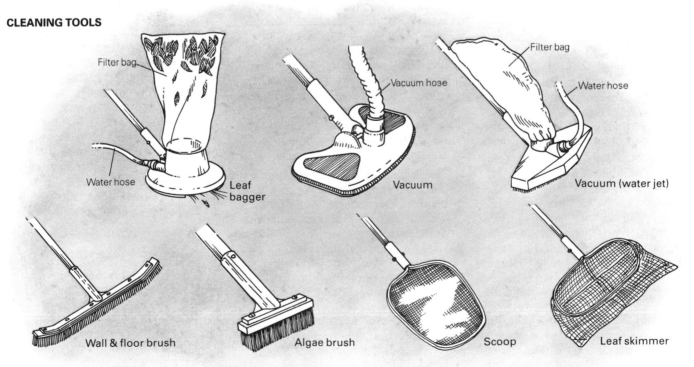

Filter bag · Water hose · Leaf bagger · Vacuum hose · Vacuum · Filter bag · Water hose · Vacuum (water jet) · Wall & floor brush · Algae brush · Scoop · Leaf skimmer

skimmer often—even every day if the wind is blowing—to remove debris before it can sink.

3. Clean the strainer baskets in the skimmer and pump (during the swimming season, clean the skimmer daily). Make sure all debris is removed so there'll be maximum suction for vacuuming.

Cover

Strainer basket

Skimmer weir

2. Clean the tile and walls. If yours is a vinyl-lined or fiberglass pool, only use cleaners recommended by the pool manufacturer. The scum line that forms on water line tile is a combination of oil and dust and usually can be cleaned off with household scouring powders and a sponge. Many companies also offer special tile cleaners that are applied with a brush. Never use steel wool to clean tile because the iron particles can stain the plaster. Remove light scale deposits from tile with a solution of muriatic acid (1 part acid to 6 parts water) or with a soft pumice stone block. If heavy scale persists, it indicates a serious water problem; call in professional help.

Brushing the pool walls requires even coverage rather than brute strength. Normally, a nylon brush is tough enough to remove the dirt that clings to the walls. You may want to brush for 10 to 15 minutes a day to make the weekly pool cleaning less of a chore. A stainless steel brush can be used periodically on plaster to dislodge algae, stubborn dirt, and calcium deposits.

Brush the walls all the way down to the floor, so the refuse can be picked up with the vacuum cleaner. Whenever possible, brush toward the main drain so some of the dirt will be pulled into the filter system as you work. Start at the shallow end and work toward the deep water. Overlap your strokes so the entire surface receives a good scrubbing.

4. Vacuum the pool at least once a week and more often if wind and rain have brought in an extra heavy dose of debris.

Operating the vacuum cleaner is not difficult; with a jet-type unit, you need only hook up a garden hose and attach the filter bag. But with a vacuum that's attached to a filtration system outlet and uses the filter pump for power, take care to eliminate any chance of air being pumped through the lines.

The vacuum hose must be completely filled with water before it's attached to the filter line; slowly submerge the line in water to eliminate air bubbles. Holding one end against a return line with the hose in the water will also work. Don't lift the vacuum head out of the water while it's in operation.

When you're operating this type of vacuum cleaner, check the filter manual to determine which valves should be closed and which should be open. For maximum suction, the only line open to the pump should be the vacuum inlet. The water level in the pool should be well above the vacuum inlet so no air can reach the fitting and enter the lines.

What is at first an awkward piece of equipment will become an efficient cleaner after a few tries. The vacuum head should be about 1/8 inch above the pool floor. Work the vacuum slowly back and forth and overlap each stroke to avoid missing any spots. Before each use of the vacuum, check the clearance and adjust the position of the wheels. If a nylon brush is part of the vacuum head, adjust it so it will touch the floor and dislodge embedded dirt. When the wheels and brush are so worn down that

they can no longer be adjusted, replace them to prevent the sharp edges of the cleaner from scratching or gouging the pool surfaces.

Try not to run fresh water into the pool while vacuuming. Do it beforehand, so you'll have the advantage of looking through still waters while working. If the sun's glare or ripples won't allow you to see the floor clearly, sprinkle some powdered tile cleaner or kitchen sink cleanser on the water and you'll be able to see through it.

It's sometimes advisable to vacuum directly to waste, if there are heavy precipitates or an unusually high soil load to be removed. Opening the waste lines of the filter will increase the suction and also cut down on maintenance of the filter media.

5. Backwash and service the filter (see page 111). The equipment will last longer when backwashed regularly and thoroughly.

6. Test the water. You'll find information on testing in the chapter "Treating Your Pool Water" beginning on page 101.

7. Add chemicals. The type and amount will depend on the test results, past experience, and anticipated use (see page 101).

8. Hose the coping and deck. Always hose the pool area before swimmers arrive or they'll track dust and dirt into the water. Keep the water spray directed away from the pool to prevent silt from being washed into the clean water. During the summer months, it's a good idea to sweep down the decking occasionally with a 5 percent chlorine solution to kill bacteria and prevent the spread of infection. (Be careful not to let the solution drain onto lawn or plantings.)

Cleaning up after a storm

A rain or wind storm can turn sparkling clear water into water that's littered, cloudy, and unfit for swimming. If you have warning of an approaching storm, cover the pool and turn on the automatic cleaner if your pool is so equipped.

If not, you'll have to go to work

after the storm with skimmer, brush, and vacuum. First, though, hose down the coping and deck. Remove all debris from the water surface with your leaf skimmer. Then brush down the walls and bottom, pushing the dirt toward the main drain. Be sure the pump is running.

Thoroughly vacuum the pool. If the vacuum leaves tracks on the sides or bottom, brush the sides and bottom again (with the pump running), while you push the dirt toward the main drain. Let the dirt settle before making another pass with the vacuum.

Cleaning the pool's accessories

The chrome-plated brass, stainless steel, and aluminum used for pool accessories require only minimum care to retain a good appearance. The surfaces out of water can be cleaned and polished with a good chrome cleaner; for underwater sections, a household cleaner can be used.

Check the diving board periodically to make sure the matting is still good and that the finish is not cracked. One major cause of board failure is water seepage into the laminations. Patching kits are available for covering small breaks in the finish.

Once a year, remove the metal ladder from its moorings and dry it completely in the sun. This will kill any algae that may be hiding around the anchor bolts or under the steps.

SUPPORT SYSTEM MAINTENANCE

Maintaining the support system—filter, pump and motor, heater, and other parts of the system—involves keeping everything in working order and watching for and correcting small problems before they develop into expensive repairs.

Follow the manufacturers' instructions and specifications when you're checking the components of the support system. If you don't have manuals for the equipment, obtain them from the manufacturers. These manuals will tell you what needs to be done, how often, and what repairs, if any, you can make yourself.

When you took delivery of your pool, the support equipment probably was sitting on a concrete slab without an enclosure. If you do enclose the equipment for protection or for esthetics, leave room for good ventilation and accessibility. Keep the enclosure neat and clean. To prolong the life of your equipment, sweep the enclosure out and wipe down the equipment every time you clean the filter.

Use the following information to establish a maintenance routine and to supplement the recommendations of the various manufacturers. Eventually, you'll be able to work out your own schedule to keep your water in pristine condition.

Caring for the filter

Three types of filters—high-rate sand, D.E. (diatomaceous earth), and cartridge—are used in home pools. To keep your pool water in good condition, the filtering media must be cleaned periodically, either by backwashing or by removing the filtering elements. Your owner's manual will recommend a procedure for your filter.

When to clean the filter. The obvious time to clean the filter is when the water is no longer clear. The best time, though, is before the quality of the water deteriorates. To determine when this best time is, look for an increase in pressure registered by a gauge on the filter tank or a decrease in water flow through the filtration system. The flow can be measured by a flow meter located on the return line.

To use the pressure method, you'll need to record the pressure reading when you start up a clean filter with clean strainer baskets in the pump and the skimmer. Depending on the filter and the rest of the system, this pressure can range from 6 to 20 psi (pounds per square inch). When the pressure has increased by 8 to 10 psi, it's time to clean the filter.

The flow meter measures the number of gallons of water per minute flowing through the system. Record the flow when starting up with a clean filter and strainer baskets. Clean the filter when the flow decreases by 20 percent.

Regardless of flow or pressure readings, you should clean your filter at least every other week.

High-rate sand filter. This filter has a valve, either slide or rotary, that controls the flow of water. If your valve is the slide type, follow the owner's manual or adjust it as needed to control the water flow described in the procedure.

To backwash a high-rate sand filter with a rotary valve, first turn the pump off (always do this when changing the valve, also). Turn the valve to the **backwash** position. This reverses the flow of water through the filter, raises the sand bed, and cleans it. The reversed flow carries the dirt and debris out through the waste line.

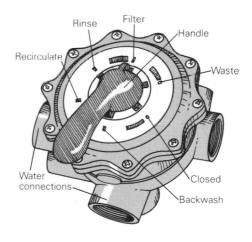

Turn the pump on and allow it to run for 2 to 3 minutes until the waste water is clear (you can watch the water through a sight glass in the filter housing). You'll now have to dispose of anywhere from 50 to 300 gallons of dirty, chlorinated water. If your community doesn't allow it to be discharged into the sewer or storm drains, you'll need a dry well to dump it.

Shut the pump off and turn the valve to the **rinse** position, allowing water to flow through the filter bed in the normal direction and into the waste line.

Turn the pump back on and run it for 15 to 20 seconds. This resets the sand bed and prevents any dirt from reentering the pool when you start filtering again.

Shut the pump off again and turn the valve to **filter,** the normal position for routing water through the filter and back into the pool. Turn the pump back on.

The rotary valve has three additional positions you may use occasionally. The **recirculate** position bypasses the filter and can be used until a leaky filter is repaired. The position marked **waste** discharges water from the pool directly into the waste line. Use this position to lower the water level or to get rid of a lot of dirt when vacuuming.

Use the **closed** position when the system is not running, such as during the winter shutdown. Never run the pump with the valve in this position.

When your pool is properly treated, your filter will require no extra maintenance. But chemical imbalance in the water can harm the filter. Water low in pH corrodes metal parts, and water high in pH and calcium precipitation can turn the sand bed into a solid chunk of scale.

If you're having to backwash your filter often and noticing inadequate filtering, scale, and dirt in the pool, open the filter and check the condition of the bed. If you find dirt deep in the sand, it's time to replace the 200 to 300 pounds of special sand.

How often you'll need to change the sand depends on the amount of dirt entering the pool; generally, it needs to be done only once a year. Your owner's manual will tell you how to do the job and how much of what type of sand you'll need.

A layer of D.E. (diatomaceous earth) ⅛ to ¼ inch thick over the sand bed will remove finer particles from the pool water. But you'll have to replace the D.E. after every backwashing. To add D.E. to your sand filter, feed a slurry of water and D.E. into the skimmer while the pump is running. You'll have to experiment to determine the correct amount.

D.E. filter. When a D.E. filter begins operating, the septa or elements supporting the filtering media must be coated with D.E., called a cake. If not, the septa, particularly the fine-textured types, will get clogged with dirt and become unusable.

To coat the septa, introduce D.E. at a fairly high-rate directly into the filter tank or as a slurry of D.E. and water into the skimmer. Run the pump while adding the D.E. Since the septa must be recoated every time you clean the filter, either a hand-fed or automatic slurry feeder will make your job easier.

If the septa in your filter have fairly wide openings, set the valve to run water from the filter to waste or directly back to the pump intake for a few minutes to prevent the pool water from becoming cloudy.

Your owner's manual explains how to clean your particular type of D.E. filter. One method is to remove the septa from the filter housing and to hose it clean; another is to backwash in a similar manner to a sand filter. In both cases, every time you clean the filter you must dispose of the old D.E. and introduce new D.E. to the septa.

To clean some filters you'll need to activate a handle that bumps the dirt and D.E. out of the septa. With this type of filter, the D.E. stays in the tank and forms a new cake when the pump is turned on. After a few bumps, though, you'll have to replace the D.E.

Cartridge filter. To clean this filter, just remove the cartridges and hose them off.

If you're using a cartridge filter on a new plaster pool, the plaster dust will clog the cartridges. Many pool builders supply an extra set of cartridges for start-up so you can throw away the first set after all the plaster dust is removed from the water.

Consult your owner's manual for detailed instructions on cleaning a cartridge filter. The procedure is very simple. If the filter is below water level, close the valve from the main drain and skimmer. Open the drain valve for the filter housing and allow water to drain out. Then open the housing and remove the cartridges.

For normal cleaning, use a high-pressure nozzle on your garden hose. Direct the water stream at an angle to the cartridge to remove the dirt.

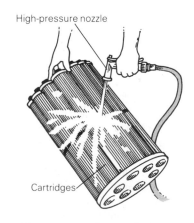

To remove oils, soak the cartridges in a plastic container in a mild solution (1 pound to 10 gallons water) of trisodium phosphate (TSP) for 1 hour. Remove them and hose them off. To remove clay, algae, or other vegetation, soak the cartridges in a strong solution (3 pounds TSP to 10 gallons water) for as long as needed. Then hose them off.

If there are calcium deposits in the cartridges, soak them in a strong solution of TSP for an hour and then rinse. Prepare a solution of 1 part muriatic acid to 20 parts water in your plastic container. CAUTION: Use eye protection and always add acid to water, not the other way around. Soak the cartridges in the acid solution until they stop bubbling. Remove them and rinse them with a hose.

Return the cartridges to the housing, replace the cover, and seal. Close the drain valve and restart the system.

Pump & motor. Considered as a single component, the pump and motor are usually purchased already assembled on the same base. The type most often used for home pools has self-lubricating bearings and seals that don't need lubricating.

The owner's manual for your pump and motor outlines the maintenance your equipment requires. Usually, you'll only need to remove hair, leaves, and other debris from the strainer basket when you vacuum the pool (see page 110) or when you've shut off the pump to clean the filter.

Have an extra basket ready to install when you remove the dirty one. Then you can clean the dirty basket at your convenience (it's easier to clean after the hair and other debris have dried).

To remove the basket, shut off the pump; if the pump is below water level, turn off the valves on the pipes from the skimmer and main drain; otherwise, you'll be doused with water when you remove the basket cover. Then remove the cover, lift out the basket, and either clean it or replace it with a spare.

After the clean basket is in

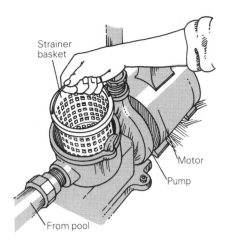

Strainer basket

Motor

Pump

From pool

place, replace the cover and tighten it securely. Open the valves on the skimmer and main drain pipes and turn the pump on. If it does not pump water immediately, shut the pump off.

Though most home pool pumps are self-priming, they may lose prime when the basket is cleaned or when there's an air leak under the basket cover or elsewhere in the system.

To prime the pump, remove the basket cover, fill the pump to brimming with water, quickly replace and secure the cover, and start the pump. Within a few seconds it should be pumping water free of air bubbles. If not, try the priming procedure one more time.

If the pump still doesn't work, call a service representative. Running a pump dry or with air entering the system can overheat and cause serious damage to both the pump and motor. Many motors have a switch that shuts off the power when the motor overheats.

Heater. Maintenance of pool heaters varies depending on the type. Check your owner's manual for the maintenance needs of your particular heater.

Generally, open-flame and electric heaters should be checked out by a competent service representative before you start up the pool in the spring. It may be necessary to disassemble the heater if there's scale in the tubes. Wire brushes or acid can usually remove the scale,

except in extreme conditions. Then the tubes have to be replaced.

Skimmer. During the swimming season, you'll need to clean the strainer basket in the skimmer daily. The basket will collect an amazing amount of debris; if it's allowed to accumulate, the debris will stop the skimming action that helps keep the water surface clean.

You don't need to shut off the pump. Simply remove the access cover to the skimmer in the pool deck and reach in and pull out the basket. Wash it off, put it back in the skimmer, and replace the cover.

SEASONAL CARE

In cold climates, you'll need to prepare your pool for the winter months and then get it ready in the spring for a new swimming season. Even in warm regions, you may not use your pool during the winter months; it, too, will require seasonal care.

Winterizing your pool

To empty or not to empty the pool? Many pool owners living in cold climates ask this question when preparing to winterize their pools.

In the days when massive poured concrete pools were common, they were emptied and the empty pools were strong and heavy enough to withstand the considerable forces exerted by wet and frozen soils. Today's pools, on the other hand, are carefully engineered to counterbalance the forces from the ground against the forces exerted by the water in the pool. And they are cheaper as a result.

Such pools can be damaged or destroyed by external pressures acting on them when they're empty. Though some disagreement remains, most pool experts concur that this danger is far greater than the pressure of ice inside a properly winterized pool.

It's now recommended that

you do not empty your pool unless it's an above-ground model with a vinyl liner. In this case, check with the manufacturer for the recommended winter protection.

Cold climate protection.   Here's how to protect your pool in areas where freezing temperatures are the rule.

Thoroughly clean and vacuum the pool (see pool cleaning method on page 109). Any dirt or debris left in the pool will dissipate the chlorine needed during the winter months. Clean the filter with a filter cleaner. If you have a problem with iron, copper, or manganese, add a sequestering agent to the water according to the manufacturer's directions.

Lower the water level by backwashing the filter to the waste line. Backwash until the waste water is crystal clear. Close the valve on the skimmer line before the water level reaches the bottom of the skimmer opening. Continue lowering the water level until the return lines are exposed.

Blow water out of all lines with the reverse flow of a tank vacuum cleaner or with an air compressor. If there's a chance that any water remains, add antifreeze. Use expandable rubber plugs to close off return lines, vacuum line, and skimmer.

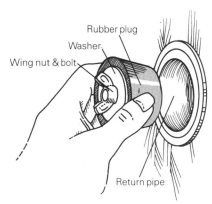

Rubber plug
Washer
Wing nut & bolt
Return pipe

Drain the water from the heater, filter, and pump. Turn off the gas to the heater and all electric power to the pump and to the rest of the pool area. Remove fuses or secure circuit breakers in the OFF position to prevent the pump from turning on accidentally.

Remove underwater lights

(some pool builders and pool service companies advocate leaving them in place). Remove the bulbs and reflectors from the lamps, and store them in a dry place. Leave the lamps face down on the deck and secure them.

Remove and clean all pool accessories, and store them indoors. Leave the diving board and slide in place (removing them would cause more damage than the winter cold). To maintain their glossy finish, coat them with a good paste wax. Chemicals and particularly the reagents in the test kit should be stored in a warm, dry place.

Use a hose to add water up to winter level—as high as possible for your pool (a few inches below the coping, or to the natural water line). Don't plug the overflow.

Test the water and add chemicals as needed. Adjust the pH to between 7.2 and 7.6 (see page 102) and superchlorinate with 10 ppm of chlorine (see page 104). Stir up any large deposits of chlorine with your pool brush to prevent discoloration of the pool finish.

Liquid chlorine will deteriorate during the winter; if you have any left, dump it in , too. Since algae will grow during the cold weather, treat the pool water with an algaecide according to the manufacturer's directions.

Cover the pool with a solid vinyl or mesh cover to eliminate laborious cleaning of your pool in the spring.

A large rubber or plastic ball or float underneath the cover will reduce freezing stress and prevent water from pooling on the solid cover. If water does accumulate, remove it with a small pump. Though the mesh cover allows more chlorine to dissipate and admits more algae-encouraging light, water won't accumulate on it.

The cover should be at least 5 feet longer and wider than the pool to protect the coping and support the snow load. Use plastic water bags to weight the edges, or tie them to anchors in the deck.

Coat any exposed metal surfaces, particularly the support

equipment, with grease or oil as protection against rust and corrosion. If the support equipment is not sheltered, loosely cover it with plastic sheeting.

Mild climate protection.   If your winters are mild, you need only to continue routine maintenance but on a reduced schedule.

Run the filter for half the time you normally run it during the swimming season. Clean the skimmer; check and adjust the pH and free chlorine once a week. Maintain the filter properly and vacuum whenever it looks dirty.

A cover over your pool will keep the pool cleaner and minimize the chlorine consumption.

Superchlorinate (see page 104) and add an algaecide before putting the cover in place. After superchlorination, the free chlorine level should be 1.0 to 3.0 ppm. If it's not, add more chlorine until this level is reached. After you cover the pool, check the chlorine level occasionally and adjust it, if necessary.

The spring opening

A pool properly maintained during the winter months can be prepared for a new season of swimming with a minimum of effort.

Hose or sweep off all dirt and debris from the cover and deck. Remove the cover and plugs from all openings. Install the underwater lights.

Turn on the electric power and start up the support system. Check for leaks and proper operation. If you find any problems, consult your owner's manual. Have the heater professionally serviced before you use it.

Test and adjust the pH and total alkalinity (see page 102). Superchlorinate and then condition (see page 104). Keep the filter running; the stabilizer may take as long as 24 hours to dissolve. Treat the water with an algaecide.

After several hours of operation, test the chlorine level and adjust it as needed. If the chlorine level is high, do not use the pool until it drops below 1.5 ppm.

A properly maintained pool should give you years of trouble-free use. But problems—whether related to water conditions or part of the support equipment—can strike any pool. If yours falls victim, let the tips below help you determine the cause and find a remedy. Be sure, too, to read the owner's manuals that came with each piece of equipment.

1. Cloudy, milky, or turbid water
- Operate filter for a longer time (see page 28)
- Backwash sand filter, recoat D.E. filter, or replace filter cartridge (see pages 111–113)
- Check and adjust chlorine, pH, and total alkalinity (see pages 102–105)
- Check for air leak in intake lines to pump (see page 118)
- Make sure filter control valve is in filter position (see page 111)
- Check skimmer and pump strainer baskets for debris (see pages 110 and 113)
- Add water clarifying agent (see pool supply or service company)

2. Green or brown cloudy water
- Algae (see page 105)

3. Cloudy or hazy water with rapid rise of pH
- Early algae growth (see page 105)

4. Brown or green slime on pool surfaces
- Algae (see page 105)

5. Black spots on pool surfaces
- Black algae (see page 105)

6. Reddish brown, brownish black, blue, or blue green water
- Metal (iron, copper, or manganese) in water (see pages 106 and 107); add sequestering agent to water (see pool supply or service company)

7. Clear green water turning to reddish brown
- Indicates iron; treat as in 6 above

8. Eye and skin irritation
- Test and adjust pH (see pages 102–103)

9. Eye and skin irritation, strong clorine smell
- Test and adjust pH; superchlorinate (see pages 102–104)

10. Low water flow
- Backwash sand filter, recoat D.E. filter, or replace filter cartridges (see pages 111–113)

- Check for air leaks in intake lines (see page 118)
- Check for restrictions in intake and return lines
- Check pump and skimmer strainer baskets for debris (see pages 110–113)
- Be sure proper valves are open
- Adjust flow valve (see owner's manual)

11. Filter needs frequent cleaning
- Check for algae; if present, see page 105
- Check and adjust chlorine and pH levels (see pages 102–103)
- Reduce flow rate in D.E. filter
- Recoat D.E. filter with finer media (see page 112)
- Clean sand filter with special cleaner (see pool supply or service company)
- Check surface of sand in sand filter; if cracked or crusted, remove 1 inch of sand

12. Heater cycles on and off
- Low water flow (see 10, above)
- Check high temperature control (see owner's manual)

13. Gas burner won't light, though pilot is on.
- Check all furnace controls (see owner's manual)
- Check that pilot flame properly heats thermocouple (see owner's manual)
- Check water pressure in heat exchanger (see owner's manual)
- Check main electric gas valve (see owner's manual)

14. Pump motor doesn't start
- Blown fuse or tripped circuit breaker (see page 119)
- Loose electrical connection or broken wire (see page 119)

15. Pump motor noisy
- Loose connections between pump and motor (see page 119)
- Worn bearing in motor (see page 119)

16. Pump runs but doesn't pump
Caution: If pump is hot, immediately shut off motor to avoid damage.
- Low water level in pool; add water
- Clogged filter—backwash sand filter, recoat D.E. filter, or replace filter cartridge (see pages 111–113)
- Air leaks in intake lines (see page 118)
- Loose pump impeller (see owner's manual)
- Pump has lost its prime (see page 113)

REPAIRING & REFURBISHING A POOL

Most well-built and well-maintained pools will last for years. But age and neglect can wear down a pool and deprive it of the sparkling luster that once made it an inviting place to swim.

Even a carefully maintained pool can show evidence of its age: decks can crack due to earth movements, the pool surface can change color, and the support system can break down. When the pool has suffered through a period of neglect, these small problems turn into major repair jobs.

Yet an old pool is not a lost investment. A few repairs—or a simple refurbishing project—may be all you need to restore the appearance and regain the enjoyment of your pool. Often, it isn't as big a task as it first appears, though most repairs require the services of an expert and can be expensive. Most people still find it cheaper to repair their pool than to replace it.

This chapter describes the pool problems you may encounter and explains the necessary repairs; you'll also find a discussion of possibilities for renewing your pool, such as adding accessories and decorative features.

Decide on the repairs or changes you need or want to make. Then determine which jobs you can do yourself. Though most repair work should be done professionally to ensure proper operation of the pool, there's much you can do. It's possible that all your pool needs is a face lifting, with new landscaping and more careful maintenance.

Repair or replace?

If your pool has deteriorated so much that repairing it will cost more than half the price of replacement, or if you have serious doubts about the quality of the original pool construction, you will probably want to replace it.

But tearing out an old concrete or fiberglass shell or removing the walls of a vinyl-lined pool is a messy and expensive job. For most people, repairing the old pool or building a new shell inside the old one is the better alternative.

Getting the job done

You'll want to have a contractor do the major repair work for you. Though in the past most contractors only built new pools, as the

number of existing pools has increased, many builders are finding that much of their business comes from pool repairs. Try to find someone who specializes in repairing older pools or at least has had some experience with it.

Choose your contractor with the same care you would use to select a builder to install a new pool (see page 82). Ask to see examples of previous repair work, and talk to the homeowners about their experiences. Be sure the operation is reputable and solvent. The contract you sign should specify all repairs to be made, an expected date of completion, and a cost estimate.

If the pool repair is part of a larger relandscaping scheme, have the contractor do the pool work before you bring in new plants or pavings that might be damaged.

TYPICAL SHELL PROBLEMS

Deterioration of the pool shell not only is unsightly but also can affect both water level and water quality. Repairs should be done as soon as possible to prevent complications. See the *Sunset* book *Basic Masonry Illustrated* for more information about masonry repairs.

Cracks

In-ground pools must withstand constantly changing pressures from movements in the surrounding soil. The pool walls may crack under the strain of these movements. Changes in water temperature, drainage problems, and structural flaws can also cause cracks.

Hairline cracks. In a concrete pool, changes in pool water temperature can produce small cracks that usually can be repaired with a single coat of paint, patching cement, a dollop of plaster, caulking compound, or epoxy putty. Force the material into the crack and smooth it down with a putty knife. Since underwater patching materials are available, it's not necessary to drain the pool (see right).

Small cracks in a fiberglass pool, on the other hand, are uncommon and may indicate a structural flaw in the shell. Call in an expert as soon as possible.

Large cracks. Large cracks in any pool may indicate a serious problem that's usually hard to repair. Two conditions are of particular

concern: cracks created by soil movement due to poor drainage and cracks brought about by inadequate pool wall construction. If you suspect either problem, you'll want to consult a soils engineer.

The only way to repair a badly constructed pool is to undo what was originally done wrong. Review your warranty to see if the repairs are covered by your pool builder.

Underwater epoxy putty
Main drain

Surface problems

A host of annoying problems can mar your pool's surface—from algae growth to spalling to scaling. Sharp objects can tear the liners of vinyl pools, and even sunlight can take its toll on a pool's color. These

problems are a nuisance, but only rarely do they present a serious problem.

Spalling plaster. For best appearance, concrete pools need to be replastered about every 10 years or repainted every 3 or 4 years. Daily contact with pool chemicals and changing pool water temperatures slowly dissolve the plaster, causing it to flake and chip.

Though spalling plaster isn't a structural danger, it does detract from the pool's appearance and can produce rough surfaces that scrape swimmers and are more likely to stain. Algae growth and scale deposits collecting on the weakened plaster contribute to more spalling.

If the damage is slight, you may be able to sand the spot and patch it with new plaster or an epoxy coating. Normal maintenance (brushing the walls) and water action will soon blend the spot into the surrounding plaster.

You can also arrest localized spalling by painting the interior of the pool. Buff all chips and blisters, wash the pool thoroughly, and then paint following the manufacturer's directions.

Do not drain the pool to work on it without a professional's assistance. A drained pool may crack or pop out of the ground.

Patching or painting a pool is

REPAIRING A CRACK

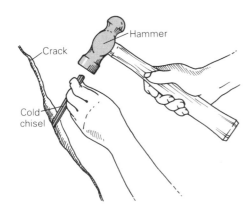

Use cold chisel to remove loose concrete and to open up and undercut sides of crack.

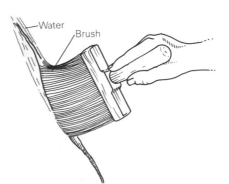

With brush, thoroughly wet surfaces of crack with water to assure that cement will bond with concrete.

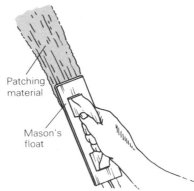

Use trowel or float to work cement patching material into crack and to smooth it flush with surface.

time-consuming but can be done by a pool owner. Obtain instructions and supplies from a pool service company or pool equipment supplier, and very carefully prepare the surface to be plastered.

If spalling is excessive, you may need to have a plasterer sandblast the old finish and replaster the pool. It's an expensive job, but it will erase all evidence of your old problems and give the pool a sparkling new face.

Lining tears. Sharp objects (or sometimes even fingernails) can tear the lining of a vinyl pool. The pool owner can repair these small tears easily. Two kinds of kits are available for fixing liners—patches and liquid sealers. Some vinyl companies even offer underwater patching kits, so you don't need to drain the pool to make repairs.

Making sound repairs to a tear longer than 2 or 3 inches is sometimes difficult. Try to repair it, but if that doesn't work, you'll want to replace the liner. Most liners are installed with special fittings that facilitate removing the old unit and installing a new one.

Like the original one, a new liner must be manufactured to fit the existing pool size and shape exactly. Since the liner must be installed accurately to prevent buckling or stretching, you'll probably want to hire a professional to do the work (see next page). If you want to replace the liner yourself, ask the manufacturer for instructions.

Discoloration. The most common pool shell problem—and the most easily repaired—are stains and color changes on pool walls. These stains usually indicate an imbalance in water chemistry leaching the color out of the walls. Refer to "Treating Your Pool Water," page 101, if you suspect a water chemistry problem is your culprit.

Sometimes, the color in the paint or plaster simply dissolves, creating a mottled effect in the pool. Though you may want to repaint or replaster a mottled pool, you can leave it as is, since the mot-

tled effect is sometimes pleasant in a naturalistic pool.

Vinyl-lined pools can be discolored by overchlorination, by chemicals applied directly on the surface without proper dilution, or by stains from a wooden sidewall. The daily bombardment of ultraviolet light from the sun can also fade the liner. You can sometimes clean a stained liner or cover the stain with a patch; a faded liner is more likely to tear and probably will have to be replaced.

Stains on the bottom of a vinyl-lined pool that don't continue up the pool sides may indicate fungal growth in the sand below the pool. The stained liner should be replaced, perhaps with one that includes an anti-fungus additive in the material, and the sand below the pool should be treated with a diluted solution of sodium hypochlorite to rid it of any fungus.

Gelcoat deterioration. Though designed to be durable, the smooth gelcoat surface on a fiberglass pool may eventually fade, chip, or change color. Gelcoat deterioration detracts from the pool's appearance but rarely constitutes a serious problem.

Most manufacturers cover gelcoat deterioration in their warranties. If the damage is localized, more gelcoat is applied over the affected areas. If the damage is widespread, it may be necessary to drain the pool and resurface the entire shell, or even replace the pool.

A coat of epoxy paint can improve the appearance of an older fiberglass pool. Be sure to follow the recommendations of the paint manufacturer; preparing the surface properly before painting is essential if the paint is to adhere.

Leaks

Leaky pool walls and pipes are the Waterloo of many pool owners. A leak is often insidious, going undetected until it has reached a serious level. Water leaking into the ground can cause major difficulties either by undermining the pool or deck or by expanding the soil so it exerts

enough pressure to crack the pool shell.

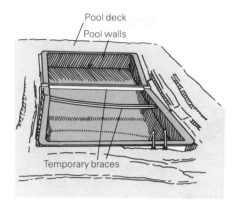
Pool deck
Pool walls
Temporary braces

Leaks are also expensive. You pay additional chemical, pumping, and heating costs to introduce new water into the system, as well as pay to replace the water itself.

Even if you know you have a leak, finding it is not easy. The leak could be anywhere—in the filter pipes, in the pool wall, or around a light or wall fitting. You may be able to locate it yourself with a leak tester, a colored fluid added to the pool that, with sufficient current, is drawn into the leak. Or you may decide to leave the job to a professional who's had experience searching for leaks.

Bulges

Bulges in the walls of vinyl-lined or fiberglass pools indicate the possibility of drainage or structural problems that need to be dealt with promptly.

In either case, the problem is a major one, requiring excavation and repair around the pool, or even replacement of sidewall panels in a vinyl-lined pool. Call in a pool professional.

Major renovation

If your pool shell has deteriorated to the point where it needs major repairs, you may want to consider building a new shell inside the old one. Treating the old pool as a big hole in the ground, your contractor builds a completely new pool in the hole; the new pool, of course, will be shallower and smaller than the original.

Though this approach avoids the hassle and expense of removing the existing pool, you can't relocate the pool or have as much design flexibility as you would by starting over. The pool shown in the lower photo on page 76 is a new-shell-in-old refurbishment; the owners were able to maintain the character of the original site and at the same time make several improvements in their pool.

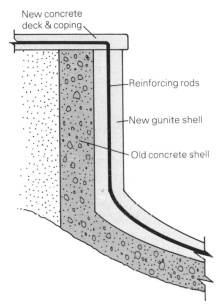

New concrete deck & coping

Reinforcing rods

New gunite shell

Old concrete shell

Another alternative is to fiberglass an existing pool or attach a vinyl liner. To fiberglass, a fiberglass mat is laid on the floor and walls of the pool and a gelcoat finish is applied to the mat's surface.

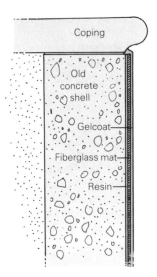

Coping

Old concrete shell

Gelcoat

Fiberglass mat

Resin

If your pool is a simple geometric shape, you may be able to fit a vinyl liner to the shell, though concrete and fiberglass pools usually require new coping and special clamps to hold the liner.

SUPPORT SYSTEM REPAIRS & REPLACEMENT

Over the years, you can almost certainly expect that some part of the mechanical support system—the pump, filter, heater, or pipes—will break down. This support equipment has a finite life and can be damaged by poor maintenance, water conditions, or the environment in which it's operating. If you're fortunate, breakdowns may be covered by your warranty.

Even in the absence of any problems, you may want to consider upgrading or replacing a piece of equipment, such as changing to a filter that's easier to clean or installing a solar heating system or a more energy-efficient pump. Consult "The Support System," page 22, and "The Solar-heated Pool," page 29, for information on the different choices available, but be sure that any new equipment meets the requirements of your pool.

Pump

The pump, the heart of the support system, circulates pool water through the filter and heater, enabling them to do their jobs. If the pump breaks down, your system will be inoperative.

Some of the most common pump problems with ideas for repairing them are listed below. You'll also want to consult your owner's manual for the pump. Though most pump repairs must be done professionally, a pool owner can make some of the basic repairs. If you think your pump is malfunctioning, turn it off; don't allow it to run dry or you can damage the pump motor.

Motor & pump malfunctions. If the motor won't start, you may have an electrical problem caused by a bad timer or switch, a loose wire, or a blown fuse or tripped circuit breaker. If the fuse is blown or the breaker is tripped, remove the cause before restarting the motor. Unless you're experienced, call in a service company for electrical problems.

Humming in a motor that won't start indicates something is jamming the inside of the pump. Remove the object and prime the pump, if needed, before restarting it.

Noise in the motor can sometimes be stopped by tightening the connections between the pump and motor. If the noise continues, the motor bearings need replacing (refer to your owner's manual). If

INSTALLING A VINYL LINER

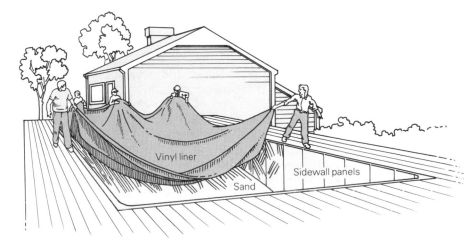

Vinyl liner

Sidewall panels

Sand

Successful installation of new vinyl liner requires several pairs of hands or professional help.

the pump is noisy, check for foreign material in the pump, and be sure the pump and motor are securely fastened to the pad.

Overheating of the pump indicates no water is passing through it. Shut the pump off immediately to avoid serious damage to the pump and motor. Check that the strainer basket isn't clogged and that no valve has been closed by mistake.

Leaks around the pump shaft indicate that the seal should be replaced (refer to your owner's manual).

Filter system

It's easy to spot a run-down filter system—leaves and debris fill the pool and the water is cloudy. Your filter may need nothing more than normal maintenance. Review the maintenance procedures for the filter on pages 111–113. Check that the strainer baskets in the skimmer and pump aren't clogged. Clean or replace your filter media or replace your cartridge.

If the problems persist, the surface area of your filter may not be large enough for your pool. Perhaps more people are now using the pool, or there's been a change in the composition of your local water. Trees around the pool may be shedding more leaves into the pool. In any case, you may have to increase the amount of chemicals you're using, run your filter longer, or replace the filter with a larger model or one of a different design.

Consider, too, the water circulation system in your pool. Are there dead spots where leaves and debris are collecting? Are the outlets adequate to carry the water to be filtered? You can add inlets and outlets to any type of pool.

Heater

Is your heater undependable as a source of heat? Does your unit require more energy to heat the pool than it once did? Most heater malfunctions result from mechanical problems, such as a breakdown of the thermostat, scale buildup in the heater lines blocking the water flow

(see below), or accumulated debris blocking air or water circulation through the heater.

A heater that's less efficient than it was in the past may have a problem with scale buildup. Water that's even slightly out of balance can allow scale to collect in the heater and block water flow. You may even see flakes of scale coming from the heater return line. If so, have a heater repair expert clean off the scale; if there's a large accumulation in an old heater, though, you may need to replace the unit.

Replacing for energy efficiency

Ever-increasing energy costs are convincing many pool owners to replace units in their support systems with more energy efficient ones. See ''The Solar-heated Pool,'' page 29, for energy-saving suggestions and equipment.

AROUND THE POOL

In the same way that soil movement can crack a pool shell, it can also pop and crack tiles around the outside of the pool and damage decks and coping. Unless it creates a safety hazard for swimmers or sunbathers, damage to tiles and decks is not of serious concern, though it can detract from the appearance of your pool.

Tile problems

The tile trim edging some pools is especially sensitive to earth movement—sometimes, it may only take an eighth of an inch of soil movement around the pool to crack or pop tile. The problem is compounded when the deck or area surrounding the pool has been built improperly, such as an uneven bond beam or a deck expanding into the pool wall.

It may be possible to re-lay the tile with a better adhesive than was used originally. But if the cracking

or popping problem is caused by faulty construction of the bond beam or deck, you'll have to dig up the area around the pool and rebuild it properly.

Deck & coping problems

Cracked paving and split expansion joints in the deck usually indicate substantial movement in the soil around your pool. But even a small movement can cause cracking, especially if your deck is constructed of several close-fitting materials expanding at different rates.

A cracked deck is not necessarily a harbinger of pool shell problems. If your pool has been solidly constructed, or if a drainage diversion underneath your deck is causing the cracking, the shell itself probably won't crack.

On the other hand, if your deck is expanding into the pool shell and putting pressure on it, you may want to have an engineering consultant advise you on how much of this pressure your pool can withstand.

Damaged coping, especially cracks and splitting at the joints between coping stones, usually indicates similar problems with earth movement. But your coping can also crack from its own expansion and contraction, if it was installed without being properly cured.

To repair hairline cracks in a concrete deck or coping, force a matching mortar or grout into the crack and smooth it even with the concrete surface. A larger crack should be chipped out and the sides of the crack undercut to hold the patching material. Cover and cure for 3 days.

If your deck is seeded with an aggregate, it's unlikely you'll be able to match the patching material to the surrounding area. Chip out a square-shaped or other defined space around the crack; lay mortar as described above, but slightly below the level of the surrounding deck. Using an aggregate that's similar in size and texture to the existing deck, sprinkle stone into the mortar, tamping down with a brick or other solid flat object.

Brush the mortar until the stones project from the surface, and wash with a light spray of water. Cover the spot and allow the mortar to cure for 3 days; you can then uncover it and wash with a diluted muriatic acid solution.

Broken bricks or other paving stones in decks or copings can be removed and replaced. Use a mortar rake or other tool to chip out the damaged stone, and replace it with one that's been cut to fit.

If the deck is severely cracked, you can build a new deck over the old one. But there are cautions to this approach. First, the new deck should be pliable to allow for continued settling in the subbase underneath. Don't simply pour more concrete over a cracked concrete deck. You can, though, lay bricks or flagstones in a bed of sand over the damaged deck, or build a new deck of wood or tile on top of it.

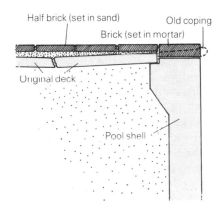

Half brick (set in sand)
Old coping
Brick (set in mortar)
Original deck
Pool shell

Secondly, continued soil settling or surfacing tree roots can also cause your deck to move vertically. If you've laid a new deck over an old one, the new deck too will be subjected to vertical pressures and damage.

If your deck does move vertically, you can usually remove the affected slabs or paving stones and either build up the area underneath or cut away the growth causing the movement. But if your deck is concrete and is severely cracked by vertical movements, you may have to tear it up and start again.

Major deck construction can put pressure on your pool; contact a pool builder first for advice on how to avoid damaging the pool shell.

Deck coatings

As your pool ages, the deck can fade or change color as dirt is ground into the surface. Slippery spots can develop from the effects of weather and algae growth.

Rather than replace the entire deck, you may choose to cover it with a deck coating or paint designed to produce an even, nonslip surface. Coatings come in a variety of colors (some match pool shell paints) and are available for most types of poolside pavings, though they're most often used on concrete decks.

REMODELING THE POOL

Is your pool in need of an up-to-date look? Do you want some of the new accessories not available when your pool was built originally? Do you need to remodel your pool to fit your changing life style? If so, some simple refurbishments of your pool and its landscape can add years of enjoyment.

Adding accessories

The most common reason to refurbish an undamaged pool is to add features designed to increase your swimming fun. All the accessories we describe can be added to an existing pool.

Diving boards and slides. You can easily add these accessories to your pool, or change to larger ones. To help avoid accidents, though, you'll want to be sure to choose the board or slide that's the right size for your pool. The NSPI provides the information you need to make this evaluation (see pages 16 and 88).

For more on diving boards and slides, see "Pool Accessories" on page 88.

Spa. The simplest way to add the warm-water advantages of a spa or hot tub to your pool is to add a detached unit, as was done for the pool shown on page 38.

If your lot isn't large enough for a separate unit or you prefer the appearance of an attached spa, you can add a custom unit at the edge of your pool. For a concrete pool, a spa can be connected to the pool wall; for a vinyl-lined or fiberglass pool, you can add a prefab spa unit.

In-shell features. Prefab fiberglass steps can be added to the shallow end of a vinyl-lined fiberglass pool; you can also have steps custom-made by a pool builder for a concrete pool. Similarly, grab rails, ladders, and swim-out steps in the deep end can be added easily.

To add lights to a vinyl-lined or fiberglass pool, you'll have to notch into the sides and possibly dig up the area around the pool for the wires. Such an installation is impossible on a concrete pool. You can though, install a special underwater light fixture on the wall of a concrete pool. Waterproof wires from the light attach to a receptacle on the deck.

Face lifting for a modern look

Perhaps your pool just looks outdated, with worn or out-of-style materials and outmoded design details. All your pool may need is a face lifting around it to bring it up to date. See "Landscaping Your Pool," page 90, for improvements you can make, such as adding a raised planting bed at the side of the pool, adding natural rock and lush plantings around the pool, building a structure for pool equipment or a cabana for seating and changing areas, and changing the materials used for the pavement.

If the pool itself looks outdated, with old coping, weathered tiles, and an uninteresting shape, examine the "Color Gallery of Pools," beginning on page 32, for some fresh approaches. Then consult a pool contractor and landscape architect—with a little work, even the most outdated pool can take on the sparkle of a new installation.

ENJOYING A SAFE POOL

How much you enjoy your pool and its surroundings depends to a large extent on your imagination in transforming the area into a center for recreation and relaxation. But your ultimate enjoyment will be determined by the rules you adopt and the methods you use to ensure the safe use of your pool.

RECREATION IN & AROUND THE POOL

Many new pool owners often say, "We just swim." But after a single season of pool use, these same people are bursting with new ideas—games they have invented, different ways to exercise, and new twists on old party ideas.

Coming up with creative ways to use your pool not only adds to your fun but also is a good way to channel in-the-pool activities in safe directions.

Water games

In-the-pool games don't have to be complicated—the water itself is enough of an attraction to satisfy most people. Always keep the ages of the players in mind. Though small children enjoy a balloon race across the width of the pool, older children demand more vigorous games, like water polo, water basketball, tag, or keep-away.

Manufactured games. Most often, these games (pictured on the next page) are in-the-pool floaters that go in the water for fun and come out when the game's over. Some are variations on standard games like volleyball and horseshoes; others are floating boards for checkers and other sedentary games. You can also purchase underwater rings for youngsters to swim through or grab and bring to the surface.

With add-ons, you can transfer almost any game into the water. If you have a favorite sport, talk to your pool designer before you build the pool to see if your game can be built in.

Homemade games. From racing floating plastic cups to installing more complicated sports equipment, your choice is as unlimited as your imagination.

You can add a basketball net to your pool, as shown on the next page. Purchase a standard backboard with ring and net (nylon nets are best since they don't deteriorate rapidly in the water and sun), and bolt it to a 1½-inch angle-iron frame that will fit the end of the diving board. Mount the frame to the board with two C-clamps.

The fishing game illustrated can keep small children occupied at the shallow end of the pool. Make fish out of metal canning lids, adding tails of plastic ribbon. Then take a dowel or stick, tie a long string from the end, and hang a magnet on the string for a hook. Drop several metal fish into the water, and let the children see who can come up with the most. Just be sure that you remove all metal from the water when the game is over.

For a little practice on more advanced fishing techniques, you can throw an old bicycle tube in the water and use it as a target for fly casting. Replace your fishing hook with a bolt or practice plug.

Exercise

Most people know that swimming is great exercise, but they don't know all the ways they can exercise in their pool. Some pools, like the lap pool on page 47 and the pool

MANUFACTURED POOL GAMES

Floating checkerboard

Ring

Weight

Ring

Floating pylon

with the current on page 78, are designed specifically for exercise.

But the shallow end of any pool can be an aquatic exercise center. Simply get in the water and do the same exercises you normally do: leg lifts, running in place, and turning at the waist. There are even advantages to exercising in the water—the buoyancy of the water prevents damage to bones and joints, and the resistance of the water helps you develop well-toned muscles.

For a well-rounded exercise program, add these aquatic exercises to lap swimming. As in any conditioning program, work up

to form slowly (especially since swimming uses more muscles than virtually any other exercise), and get professional advice if you have a medical condition.

Entertainment

Relaxing at poolside with friends after an exhilarating swim may be the most enjoyable part of your day—or evening. Since swimming encourages ravenous appetites, such gatherings usually include eating.

A patio barbecue or fireplace will take care of the cooking, but the dining facilities require some at-

tention. You'll probably want to separate diners from the pool as much as possible, since they won't relish the splashing from the pool. A 15-foot deck width between the pool and the dining table is ideal, but if conditions are crowded, screens and plantings can isolate the dining area from the pool.

Heating the poolside may not be the most efficient use of energy, but it can allow you to enjoy the area on cool summer evenings and extend its use into spring and autumn months. You can warm the poolside with a firepit, barbecue, brazier, fireplace, or infrared heater.

HOMEMADE POOL GAMES

Basketball backboard & net

Wood support

C-clamp

Diving board

Bicycle inner tube

Horseshoe magnet

Steel jar lid

A firepit serves multiple functions—it gives off good light, can double as a barbecue, and, fueled by wood or gas, is a good heat source as well. A brazier with an open or screened side and a built-in barbecue can provide some heat, but a portable barbecue or brazier you can move to where quick heat is needed is even better. Burn charcoal instead of wood to eliminate eye-stinging smoke.

A large fireplace, if space permits, or a portable one can produce generous amounts of heat. But a portable fireplace made from pottery can crack if you try to build a roaring fire in it, so burn only small amounts of kindling wood.

You can also heat the pool area with an infrared heater fueled with natural or propane gas or with electricity. These are most effective in sheltered areas. Though usually permanently mounted, you can put a heater with its own propane tank on wheels and roll it to wherever you want the heat.

Be careful to keep open fires away from trees and shrubs, patio roofs, and other wood structures that can be ignited by wind-blown sparks and firebrands. Cover the fire with a screen to reduce the effects of the wind.

RULES FOR SAFE POOL USE

Along with a pool come some weighty responsibilities you'll want to give serious thought to. What features are necessary to ensure safe pool use? Where should the line be drawn on roughhousing? How can the pool accommodate tots, teenage splashers, and serious swimmers at the same time?

To answer these questions, you'll want to consider who will be using the pool and what rules you will need to adopt in order to guarantee fun and safety for everyone.

Unfortunately, pool owners all too often wait for some incident or accident before setting guidelines. Establish your rules before the first person steps into your pool, or, bet-

ter yet, before construction begins. You can always adjust them later.

If possible, make sure that everyone using the pool has had training in water safety and basic rescue methods. Check with your local chapter of the American Red Cross for information on classes given in your community.

The Red Cross publishes a booklet, *Basic Rescue and Water Safety,* which gives information on assisting a swimmer in difficulty, artificial respiration, first aid for swimmers, family water safety, and survival floating, among other subjects. *Lifesaving: Rescue and Water Safety,* also published by the Red Cross, covers all aspects of rescue and water safety in detail.

Obtain clear instructions for mouth-to-mouth resuscitation, learn the techniques, and teach them to everyone who will be using your pool. It is imperative to have the instructions posted in the pool area—though you may once have learned how to perform mouth-to-mouth resuscitation, the techniques can be quickly forgotten. The Red Cross offers a waterproof instruction sheet that will withstand weather, along with other printed guides for poolside safety.

Post your pool rules and emergency phone numbers. Keep a first

aid kit and basic lifesaving equipment at hand. Important lifesaving aids are a life ring with rope attached and a rescue hook, both of which are illustrated below. The long, blunt-ended pole used for brushing the sides of the pool can be extended quickly to faltering swimmers.

The safety guidelines you'll want to set should include determining who can use the pool and when, what behavior is acceptable—and unacceptable— in and around the pool, and what maintenance standards are necessary to keep pool facilities safe.

You may think that the sample guidelines that follow are common sense, but don't assume that your neighbors or your children will follow them without being reminded. Take the time to review these and other basic rules with the people using your pool.

Who can swim & when?

While your pool is being installed, you may find that not only your own but also your neighbors' excitement and expectations will be at a peak. This turn of events may both please and bewilder you—though you're probably quite willing to share the pool with neighbors, you

LIFESAVING EQUIPMENT

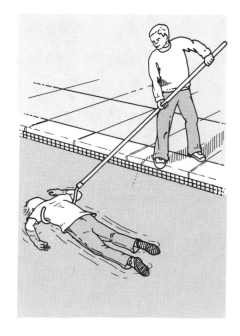
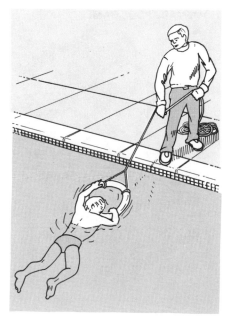

may not know how to go about it.

The problem can be more complicated if you're moving into a house that already has a pool, since neighbors may be accustomed to having free access to it whenever they want.

In either case, the pool is your responsibility. To prevent mishaps and misunderstandings, you'll want to set guidelines from the beginning for who can use the pool and when.

Nonswimmers.   Keep any adults or children who don't know how to swim a safe distance away from the edge of the pool. Allow only one nonswimming child, accompanied by an adult who knows how to swim, into the shallow end of the pool at a time. Be sure any other nonswimming children are sufficiently away from the pool to be out of danger.

You may want to tie a floating rope across the pool where it begins to deepen to be sure that non-swimmers don't go in over their heads. Even partially skilled swimmers should always have one-to-one supervision, since they may overestimate their swimming skills or panic and forget how to handle themselves in the water.

No swimming alone.   Never permit anyone in your pool, or even near it, when no one else is around. A responsible adult who knows how to swim should always be present when anyone is in the water. Don't leave—even for a few minutes—since suddenly unsupervised children often take chances that may endanger them.

Don't even let adults swim alone. People who are drowning rarely call out for help or make enough noise to bring assistance. Add an outdoor telephone outlet so you don't have to leave the pool area for calls.

Health rules.   Sick people should stay out of the pool since bacteria and infections can spread quickly in the water. No one with a cold, earache, infected cuts, open sores, or any other ailment should go into

the water. Children will sometimes conceal an illness so they can be part of the fun; be sure that children using your pool understand the importance of staying out of the water if they aren't feeling well.

Do not allow any eating or drinking for an hour before swimming. Not only is there a danger of swimmers coming down with debilitating cramps, but there is also evidence that more than half the adults who drown each year in pool accidents are intoxicated.

Encourage rest periods of 10 to 15 minutes every hour to calm excited children and to settle the nerves of supervising adults.

Handling guests.   You may want to allow neighbors and friends to use your pool by invitation only. Some pool owners set up certain hours for different age groups, reserving early evenings and weekends for adult relaxation. If neighbors arrive in their bathing suits with their own towels, it will curb dressing-room confusion and eliminate their tracking through the house.

Limit the number of people who can be in the pool area at one time. A swimmer in danger can easily go unnoticed amidst the noise and confusion of an over-crowded pool; the presence of a lot of people can also lead to rough-housing and encourage some swimmers to show off and take dangerous chances.

Pool preparation.   Before anyone enters the pool, be sure that all preparatory steps have been completed. The pool cover should be competely removed, since swimmers can be caught below the cover and can drown in even a partially covered pool. The water should be in correct chemical balance, and all leaves, debris, and foreign objects should be removed.

When not to swim.   Thunderstorms endanger swimmers—keep people away from the pool when there's a chance of lightning.

Do not allow nighttime swimming unless you planned for it in

your original pool design. You need enough light in and around the pool so a swimmer can be spotted easily; don't swim at night if any of the lights are not working.

Safety in & around the pool

Once you've determined who can safely use the pool, you'll want to set some guidelines to be sure they use it in a safe manner. Post these rules in a prominent place to remind swimmers—and their supervisors—that safety is important.

Behavior around the pool. Impress on children that the pool area is only for swimming and supervised play and that they should never enter the pool area unless an adult who knows how to swim is present.

Do not permit any running, pushing, or horseplay around or in the pool. At times you may feel like you're fighting a hopeless battle. Many children are full of unrestrained activity at poolside and forget even the most basic rules. It's one of the reasons that constant supervision is so important, and also a good reason for organizing poolside games to channel all that energy.

Diving & sliding.   Reckless diving can easily cause serious injury. If you have a diving board, allow only one person at a time to jump or dive off the front of the board. Divers should keep their dives simple— the boards used in home pools are not for Olympic-style diving.

If you don't have a board, permit diving only into the deep end and then only if your pool is more than 6 feet deep. Expert divers need to be especially cautious; less experienced divers may actually be safer because their imprecise movements create drag that slows their underwater descent.

Water slides, similarly, are designed for one person at a time and always feet first in a seated position. Whether sliding or diving, the right-of-way always belongs to the swimmer already in the water. If people are diving or sliding into the pool when others are swimming, try to keep the activities as separate as possible.

Some of the most severe pool-related injuries occur from using slides. Always observe three rules on slides: stay seated, slide down in a feet-first position, and beware of hitting your feet on the pool bottom (leg fractures can result).

Avoiding sudden water hazards. Hyperventilation often starts innocently enough; a swimmer simply takes several deep breaths before a long swim underwater. This oxygen overdose forces carbon dioxide out of the lungs and blood, so the brain never gets the message that the swimmer needs to come up for more air.

A swimmer suffering from hyperventilation can suddenly black out underwater and drown if not brought to the surface and given mouth-to-mouth resuscitation. Discourage swimmers from taking extended swims underwater.

Floating rafts, balls, and other play equipment can carry unqualified swimmers into water that's too deep for their abilities. If the equipment pops suddenly or the rider slips off, there's potential for tragedy. Do not allow a nonswimmer or semiskilled swimmer to play on such inflatables—it's probably better to leave them out of the pool until everyone is a qualified swimmer.

Hazards around the pool. Keep refreshments completely away from the pool. This applies to everyone, since adults can also be careless. It only takes one broken glass to cover the deck or the floor of the pool with dangerous fragments—and glass is the most difficult material to see and clean up. Use only unbreakable glasses or plates at poolside, and, since you want to discourage eating and drinking before dunking, serve food only in areas away from the pool.

Electrical appliances, including radios, used in the pool area must be properly grounded to avoid the possibility of electric shock and need to be kept away from the splashing of the pool. Keep all

extension cords well away from the water, and immediately repair any damage to outdoor wiring.

All electrical outlets, as well as the circuits for the support equipment, must be protected by ground-fault interrupter circuit breakers to prevent injuries. (see the *Sunset* book *Basic Home Wiring Illustrated*).

Maintaining the pool. If not properly maintained, even the most carefully designed pool can become a hazard. Check your pool area frequently for developing problems and make repairs before they get out of control.

Ask neighbors and friends who use the pool frequently to help with clean-up and maintenance chores. Decks should be cleaned of all debris and slippery spots removed. Broken drain covers in the pool can trap swimmers in the suction. Don't allow anyone to swim in a pool with a damaged drain cover until it's repaired.

Safety fences, pool covers, & alarms

In addition to following the NSPI standards (see page 16) for the design of the pool itself, you may want to add a fence, cover, or alarm to keep unsupervised children and uninvited adults away from the water.

Never underestimate the lengths to which toddlers will go to get into the pool. Not old enough to have learned a healthy respect for the possibility of poolside accidents, these children will climb trees, jump over walls, or set up Rube Goldberg-like combinations of boxes and chairs as makeshift ladders to scale fences.

Fences. When designing poolside fencing to protect children, keep in mind the following considerations:
• Toddlers and small children are usually safe behind a 4½-foot fence, but older children need one that's at least 5 or 6 feet high. Even that height may not deter them.
• Construct the fence out of

an unclimbable material with no toeholds in the frame. A 1 by 2-inch wire mesh works well. The fence should be open enough so the pool can be seen from the house.
• Garbage cans, lawn furniture, and other objects that can be used to scale the fence should be out of reach. Locate the fence away from trees that can be climbed.
• Keep gates into the pool area locked.

Inspect the fences around your pool or property often. Rainwater or burrowing animals can dig away the bases; these depressions may be large enough for a child to crawl through.

Pool covers. You may consider installing a pool cover like those shown on page 53 and in the upper photo on page 65 as one way to keep toddlers out of the water. Both covers operate automatically and cover the pool with sturdy surfaces that shouldn't break under a child's weight. Though they provide an extra measure of protection, don't use them as a substitute for fencing. Solar blankets and other covers, depending on the material, will give some protection if fastened securely to the deck.

Alarms. Alarms are not commonly used alone for safety, since they afford no protection when there's no one around to hear the buzzer. But if you have small children, an alarm is one way to be sure they aren't playing near the pool when you can't keep an eye on them.

Some alarm systems have sensing mechanisms that are triggered by an object falling into the water. Nothing sounds until something (or somebody) hits the water—and is possibly already in trouble. Other systems set up a beam around the perimeter of the pool and activate an alarm when something breaks the beam—including moths, butterflies, and even intense fog.

Alarm systems are only worthwhile if they're operating; consult the manufacturer's instructions and check the system periodically.

GLOSSARY

Defined below are the words and terms you'll need to know as a swimming pool owner.

Acid demand: amount of acid required to lower pH and total alkalinity of pool water to correct level.

Algae: minute plant life growing in water in the presence of sunlight and carbon dioxide.

Algaecide: chemical that kills algae.

Algistat: chemical that inhibits algae growth.

Alkalinity: amount of bicarbonate, carbonate, or hydroxide compounds in water.

Ammonia: chemical compound of nitrogen and hydrogen that combines with free chlorine in pool water to form chloramine; chloramine causes burning eyes, skin irritation, and chlorine odor.

Available chlorine: free or combined chlorine used to disinfect pool water.

Backfilling: filling space between pool shell and sides of excavation with dirt.

Backwashing: cleaning pool filter by reversing water flow.

Bacteria: microscopic organisms not always conducive to a healthful pool.

Breakpoint: time when increasing level of chlorine in pool water kills germs and bacteria by oxidizing all organic matter.

Calcium hypochlorite: chemical compound of calcium and chlorine (also called dry chlorine) used to disinfect water; releases 70 percent of its weight as available chlorine.

Cartridge: disposable element containing filtering media and used in some pool filters.

Chloramine: see Ammonia.

Chlorine demand: amount of chlorine needed to oxidize all organic material in pool water at a given moment or over a period of time.

Chlorine residual: amount of chlorine remaining in pool water after chlorine demand has been satisfied; oxidizes any additional organic material entering pool.

Chlorinated isocyanurate: chlorine and cyanuric acid compound used to maintain chlorine level in pool water and prevent chlorine from dissipating in sunlight. See Conditioned water.

Coagulant: chemical compound, usually alum, used in pool water to gather and precipitate out suspended matter. See Floc.

Combined chlorine: chlorine combined with other substances; though available to disinfect pool water, chlorine in this form is less effective than free chlorine.

Conditioned water: water treated with cyanuric acid or chlorinated isocyanurate to prevent chlorine from dissipating in sunlight.

Corrosion: chemical reaction that causes deterioration of metal.

Cyanuric acid: acid used in pool water to prevent chlorine loss.

Diatomaceous earth (D.E.): sedimentary rock composed of microscopic skeletons of diatoms.

Diatomaceous earth (D.E.) filter: pool filter using D.E. as filtering medium.

Disinfectant: chemical (also called bacteriacide) used to destroy germs and bacteria.

Electrolysis: flow of electrical current through acidic liquid or damp earth; corrodes metals.

Filter: device for removing suspended particles from pool water.

Filter cycle: time of filter operation between backwashes.

Filter media: fine-grain materials in filter trap matter suspended in pool water.

Filter septa: elements in D.E. filter on which D.E. is suspended.

Floc: gel-like substance formed when coagulant, usually alum combines with suspended alkaline matter in pool water and precipitates out.

Hardness: quantity of dissolved minerals, such as calcium and magnesium, in pool water.

Muriatic acid: a dilute solution of hydrochloric acid used to lower alkalinity and clean masonry surfaces.

pH: measure of acidity or alkalinity of water; pH of 7 is neutral, below 7 is acidic, and above 7 alkaline.

ppm: parts per million (in a pool, parts of a chemical or mineral per million parts of water, by weight).

Precipitate: insoluble compound formed when chlorine or alum added to pool water reacts with other chemicals or minerals.

Residual: see Chlorine residual.

Sand filter: pool filter using sand as filtering medium.

Scale: hard deposit of minerals on heater coils and pool surfaces.

Skimmer: device that continuously draws surface water and surface debris into filtration system.

Skimmer weir: part of skimmer that adjusts to small changes in water level and assures continuous flow of water into skimmer.

Soda ash: sodium carbonate used to raise alkalinity of pool water.

Sodium bicarbonate: baking soda used to raise total alkalinity of pool water with little change in pH.

Sodium bisulfate: dry acid that, mixed with water, lowers pH and total alkalinity of pool water.

Sodium hypochlorite: liquid containing 12 to 15 percent available chlorine used to disinfect pool water.

Strainer basket: device in skimmer and input side of pump used to catch large pieces of debris in pool water.

Superchlorination: heavy dose of chlorine added to pool water to burn out nitrogen compounds when bacteria, algae, or ammonia build-up cannot be reduced by normal treatment.

Swimming load: number of people using pool at a given time.

Total alkalinity: amount of alkali salts in pool water.

Turbidity: degree to which pool water is clouded by suspended matter.

Turnover rate: number of times all the pool water passes through filter in a given time period.

INDEX

Boldface numerals refer to photographs.